Day Wal
Cotswol

20 classic circular routes

Vertebrate Publishing, Sheffield
www.v-publishing.co.uk

Day Walks in the Cotswolds

20 classic circular routes

Written by
Judy Mills

Day Walks in the Cotswolds

20 classic circular routes

VP First published in 2017 by **Vertebrate Publishing.**

Vertebrate Publishing, Crescent House, 228 Psalter Lane,
Sheffield S11 8UT, United Kingdom.
www.v-**publishing**.co.uk

A CIP catalogue record for this book is available from the British Library.

ISBN 978-1-910240-99-1

Front cover: Crickley Hill, by Barrow Wake (route 13).
Back cover: St Andrew's Church, Chedworth (route 9).
Photography by **Adam Long.** www.adamlong.co.uk

Design by Nathan Ryder, production by Jane Beagley.
www.v-**publishing**.co.uk

Printed and bound in Europe by Pulsio.
Vertebrate Publishing is committed to printing on paper from sustainable sources.

Contents

* Shortcut available

CLASSIC COTSWOLDS COTTAGE IN BLEDINGTON (ROUTE 3)

Introduction

With many popular and picturesque villages such as Broadway, Bourton-on-the-Water and Castle Combe, the Cotswolds attracts day trippers of all ages, but a short walk from most of these hubs reveals small hamlets with historic houses and churches and meandering streams flowing into small rivers, once turning the machinery for woollen mills in the valley bottoms. To the west and south, climbing the often-steep slopes out of the valleys, there are views over many counties from the windswept hilltops, often boasting their own monument or tower, or ancient earthwork, burial mound or hill fort. Further east the terrain is much flatter, yet still full of character and history.

With eyes and ears open, it is unlikely that any of the walks could be completed without seeing kestrel, buzzard, red kite, heron or woodpecker; roe deer or muntjac, rabbit, hare and perhaps fox and badger. In spring and summer, limestone-loving wild flowers abound, while even out of season the flora of the Cotswolds has its own beauty, berried or frost-rimed.

All the walks in this book are within the Cotswolds Area of Outstanding Natural Beauty (AONB) and part of a limestone outcrop which extends both further north and south. The AONB reaches from south of the city of Bath north-north-east to include much of Gloucestershire and parts of Wiltshire, with spurs into Oxfordshire, Worcestershire and Warwickshire.

The walker in the Cotswolds can choose to forge on and cover the ground, stretch their legs, arrive breathless at the top of a hill and move on down into the next valley, or they can take time to explore and visit the many churches, using them like punctuation marks throughout the walk. Read the inscriptions and information boards; look ahead of your footfall for the butterfly orchids and herb Paris; take in the atmosphere of the less-visited villages, their cottages and gardens. Wonder or just smile at the quaint place names – Hetty Pegler's Tump, Lower Slaughter, Barrow Wake, Owlpen, Ozleworth Bottom. It's all there waiting for you.

Judy Mills

Acknowledgements

The author is grateful to the following who helped in the preparation of this book:

My family, Eddy and Ed Mills, who checked some of the walks and tolerated months of living with maps spread on every available surface. Both gave encouragement and moral support. Heather Wilcox who did so many of the walks with me that she now needs new boots. Brecon the springer spaniel who tested the dog-friendliness of stiles, gates and pubs. Most of all Lily Dyu who put me in touch with the team at Vertebrate Publishing. May her own writings soon be in print as they deserve.

About the walks

The day walks in this book are divided geographically into three sections and then listed in ascending order of distance. This does not necessarily mean that the longest distance walks will take the longest time. All are designed as 'day' walks inasmuch as it is not intended that anyone will attempt more than one in a day.

Walk times

Stating the obvious, walkers' fitness levels, walking speeds and interests all vary and the time given is very approximate. Some walkers will want to visit every church, look in shops, take photographs and spend awhile at a lunch stop. Perhaps the best advice is to try one of the shorter walks, starting early enough so that you aren't caught out after dark; compare your time with the time suggested, then adjust times accordingly.

Navigation

This book refers to Ordnance Survey 1:25,000-scale maps of which six have been used. It should not be necessary to refer to one of these while walking; the book map and directions should be sufficient. However, some walkers may wish or need to vary the routes, which is when the OS map will be required. In most cases the compass points are not used in route descriptions, but having a compass handy is not a bad idea.

The six OS maps in the 1:25,000 *Explorer* series are:
Explorer OL45, The Cotswolds
Explorer 155, Bristol & Bath
Explorer 167, Thornbury, Dursley & Yate
Explorer 168, Stroud, Tetbury & Malmesbury
Explorer 179, Gloucester, Cheltenham & Stroud
Explorer 190, Malvern Hills & Bredon Hill

The following 1:50,000-scale map in the *Landranger* series may come in handy on walk 14:
Landranger 163, Cheltenham & Cirencester

GPS and mobile phones

Newfangled things that the author can usually live without. Both have their place but neither can be relied upon. Quite seriously, despite the Cotswolds being a civilised area, there are many places where there is no phone reception and many wooded stretches where your GPS will lose signal. Remember to charge the batteries!

Parking

The start of most walks is from roadside or lay-by parking and therefore free of charge. There is one exception where donations are requested (Notgrove, walk 4); here they also request that walking parties (size not defined but presumably several cars) do not park there except by prior arrangement. Please park considerately and never obstruct gateways, taking into consideration that access may be needed for large tractors towing equally large trailers.

Rights of way

Rights of way have been taken from the Ordnance Survey 1:25,000 maps. For the most part, paths, including permissive paths, are marked on the ground with appropriate signage. All these are, however, subject to change. Where signs ask you to walk around rather than through a crop or livestock, please respect the landowner's wishes.

Safety

In general, the Cotswolds is kind. It's not rugged, wild country, but rolling agricultural land. However, even here, planning can help to prevent incidents and accidents. Winter walking is enjoyable, but immobility caused by a fall could soon result in hypothermia. Wear suitable footwear. Always ensure you have sufficient warm clothing, and, especially if walking alone, consider a whistle and emergency blanket or bivvy bag which will take very little space in your rucksack.

The weather can change quickly and unexpectedly; if you are in any doubt, it's probably best not to start, and if you do get caught out, it's always better to back off your route rather than carry on regardless. The hills will always be there. In winter, consider carrying a torch in case the light fades before you get off the hill – it's difficult reading a map in the dark.

Rescue

In the case of an emergency dial **999** and ask for **Police** and then **Search and Rescue**. Where possible give a six-figure grid reference of your location or that of the casualty. If you don't have mobile reception where you are, try and attract the help of others around you. The usual distress signal is six short blasts on a whistle every minute. If you don't have a whistle, then shouting may work.

Emergency rescue by SMS text

Another option in the UK is contacting the emergency services by SMS text – useful if you have a low battery or intermittent signal, but you do need to register your phone first. To register, simply text **'register'** to **999** and then follow the instructions in the reply. **Do it now** – it could save yours or someone else's life. **www.emergencysms.org.uk**

NYMPSFIELD LONG BARROW, COALEY PEAK (BY ROUTE 19)

The Countryside Code

Respect other people

Please respect the local community and other people using the outdoors. Remember your actions can affect people's lives and livelihoods.

Consider the local community and other people enjoying the outdoors

» Respect the needs of local people and visitors alike – for example, don't block gateways, driveways or other paths with your vehicle.

» When riding a bike or driving a vehicle, slow down or stop for horses, walkers and farm animals and give them plenty of room. By law, cyclists must give way to walkers and horse riders on bridleways.

» Co-operate with people at work in the countryside. For example, keep out of the way when farm animals are being gathered or moved and follow directions from the farmer.

» Busy traffic on small country roads can be unpleasant and dangerous to local people, visitors and wildlife – so slow down and where possible, leave your vehicle at home, consider sharing lifts and use alternatives such as public transport or cycling. For public transport information, phone Traveline on 0871 200 22 33 or visit **www.traveline.info**

Leave gates and property as you find them and follow paths unless wider access is available

» A farmer will normally close gates to keep farm animals in, but may sometimes leave them open so the animals can reach food and water. Leave gates as you find them or follow instructions on signs. When in a group, make sure the last person knows how to leave the gates.

» Follow paths unless wider access is available, such as on open country or registered common land (known as 'open access' land).

» If you think a sign is illegal or misleading such as a *Private – No Entry* sign on a public path, contact the local authority.

» Leave machinery and farm animals alone – don't interfere with animals even if you think they're in distress. Try to alert the farmer instead.

» Use gates, stiles or gaps in field boundaries if you can – climbing over walls, hedges and fences can damage them and increase the risk of farm animals escaping.

» Our heritage matters to all of us – be careful not to disturb ruins and historic sites.

Protect the natural environment

We all have a responsibility to protect the countryside now and for future generations, so make sure you don't harm animals, birds, plants or trees and try to leave no trace of your visit. When out with your dog make sure it is not a danger or nuisance to farm animals, horses, wildlife or other people.

Leave no trace of your visit and take your litter home

- Protecting the natural environment means taking special care not to damage, destroy or remove features such as rocks, plants and trees. They provide homes and food for wildlife, and add to everybody's enjoyment of the countryside.
- Litter and leftover food doesn't just spoil the beauty of the countryside, it can be dangerous to wildlife and farm animals – so take your litter home with you. Dropping litter and dumping rubbish are criminal offences.
- Fires can be as devastating to wildlife and habitats as they are to people and property – so be careful with naked flames and cigarettes at any time of the year. Sometimes, controlled fires are used to manage vegetation, particularly on heaths and moors between 1 October and 15 April, but if a fire appears to be unattended then report it by calling **999**.

Keep dogs under effective control

When you take your dog into the outdoors, always ensure it does not disturb wildlife, farm animals, horses or other people by keeping it under effective control. This means that you:

- keep your dog on a lead, or
- keep it in sight at all times, be aware of what it's doing and be confident it will return to you promptly on command
- ensure it does not stray off the path or area where you have a right of access

Special dog rules may apply in particular situations, so always look out for local signs – for example:

- dogs may be banned from certain areas that people use, or there may be restrictions, byelaws or control orders limiting where they can go
- the access rights that normally apply to open country and registered common land (known as 'open access' land) require dogs to be kept on a short lead between 1 March and 31 July, to help protect ground-nesting birds, and all year round near farm animals

» at the coast, there may also be some local restrictions to require dogs to be kept on a short lead during the bird breeding season, and to prevent disturbance to flocks of resting and feeding birds during other times of year

It's always good practice (and a legal requirement on 'open access' land) to keep your dog on a lead around farm animals and horses, for your own safety and for the welfare of the animals. A farmer may shoot a dog which is attacking or chasing farm animals without being liable to compensate the dog's owner.

However, if cattle or horses chase you and your dog, it is safer to let your dog off the lead – don't risk getting hurt by trying to protect it. Your dog will be much safer if you let it run away from a farm animal in these circumstances and so will you.

Everyone knows how unpleasant dog mess is and it can cause infections, so always clean up after your dog and get rid of the mess responsibly – 'bag it and bin it'. Make sure your dog is wormed regularly to protect it, other animals and people.

Enjoy the outdoors

Even when going out locally, it's best to get the latest information about where and when you can go. For example, your rights to go on to some areas of open access land and coastal land may be restricted in particular places at particular times. Find out as much as you can about where you are going, plan ahead and follow advice and local signs.

Plan ahead and be prepared

You'll get more from your visit if you refer to up-to-date maps or guidebooks and websites before you go. Visit **www.gov.uk/natural-england** or contact local information centres or libraries for a list of outdoor recreation groups offering advice on specialist activities.

You're responsible for your own safety and for others in your care – especially children – so be prepared for natural hazards, changes in weather and other events. Wild animals, farm animals and horses can behave unpredictably if you get too close, especially if they're with their young – so give them plenty of space.

Check weather forecasts before you leave. Conditions can change rapidly especially on mountains and along the coast, so don't be afraid to turn back. When visiting the coast check for tide times on **www.ukho.gov.uk/easytide** – don't risk getting cut off by rising tides and take care on slippery rocks and seaweed.

Part of the appeal of the countryside is that you can get away from it all. You may not see anyone for hours, and there are many places without clear mobile phone signals, so let someone else know where you're going and when you expect to return.

Follow advice and local signs

England has about 190,000km (118,000 miles) of public rights of way, providing many opportunities to enjoy the natural environment. Get to know the signs and symbols used in the countryside to show paths and open countryside.

SUDELEY CASTLE (ROUTE 14)

Dogs

Always keep your dog under close control, if not actually on a lead. Don't convince yourself that your pet won't chase animals; it's a natural instinct. Farmers have a right to shoot dogs that are worrying livestock or 'at large' (not under close control) in a field of sheep: remember, especially over hilly terrain, there may be animals just over the brow and the field may not be as empty as it first appears. Clear up after your dog, and take the bag away with you: dog waste bins are a rarity except in built-up areas. And remember that some people don't like or are even scared of dogs, and calling 'he won't hurt you' won't change that.

In wider forest and woodland areas, landowners such as the Forestry Commission and the National Trust suggest using 'stick and flick' instead of bagging your dog waste. Using a stick to flick it into the undergrowth allows it to decompose naturally while removing it from the path. Obviously around buildings, sports areas and roads, it should be bagged and disposed of as suggested in the Countryside Code.

Farmland

Over eighty-five per cent of the Cotswolds AONB is farmland. This means that a lot of the time you will be walking through someone's private yet beautiful factory. Just as if you were walking through a workshop, please treat it with respect: 'just grass' is animal feed, so never leave anything that could be ingested by livestock. Don't meddle with machinery; respect all fences, walls and hedges; leave open gates open, but if you open it, close it behind you. Try to give animals a wide berth; don't get too close to, and never between, a cow and her young calf. Don't damage crops and don't be tempted to take maize cobs or swedes home for your tea – they may have recently been sprayed with chemicals and, anyway, it's theft.

Other users of the countryside

Responsible and considerate use of the countryside means that everyone can work and play together, and having respect for others makes for a more enjoyable experience.

If you are unfamiliar with driving on narrow country roads, be prepared to pull in to let others pass. Drive slowly past horses and pedestrians, giving them plenty of room. Don't try to force your way through herds of cattle or flocks of sheep being driven on roads – it's better to stop and allow them to pass in their own time, and don't be tempted to sound your horn at them.

When walking on roads, keep to the right except on blind bends. Keep dogs and children under control. Remember that country roads are frequently muddy or (when icy) ungritted, and even though it may be your right of way, don't expect vehicles to stop or change course in an instant.

Country people are used to talking to those they meet. Whether they are mending a wall, grooming a horse or cleaning a church, a 'hello' is common courtesy, and often they have information or stories that will make your walk more interesting.

The Cotswold Way (and other long distance paths)

The Cotswold Way runs between Chipping Campden in the north and Bath Abbey to the south; a meandering distance of around 102 hilly miles mostly along the western edge of the Cotswolds. To have made a point of avoiding the path in this book would have been to miss some Cotswold gems. Over the years, improvements in signing, if not in surface, have made this an easy-to-follow linear path for those with several days at their disposal.

Several other recognised trails now run through the Cotswolds which all together means signposting is better and route finding much easier than it used to be. These include the Darcy D'Alton Way, the Monarch Way, the Diamond Way, the Windrush Way, the Warden's Way, the Gloucestershire Way, the Laurie Lee Wildlife Way and even the Gustav Holst Way. The Macmillan Way, 290 miles from Boston, Lincolnshire, to Abbotsbury, Dorset, is used by many to raise funds for Macmillan Cancer Support: walkers in green T-shirts with collection boxes will be grateful for any donations.

How to use this book

This book should provide you with all the information you need for a series of enjoyable walks, but there is still the need for careful planning. Once you have decided which route to follow, read the information carefully and make sure that you have sufficient time to return to your car before dark. Check the directions against the map, then you will have an idea of what to expect.

Six separate OS 1:25,000 maps cover the area within this book (see page ix), so buying them all will not be cheap, but consider taking the complete map in case you need to cut short your walk or make your way to a town or village.

The countryside is alive. Trees are planted or saplings seed; they grow, mature and fall or are felled. Hedges may be planted or grubbed-out. Fences, stiles, gates and even walls change. The book descriptions may not match the features on the ground. If this happens, a reference to the map should make clear the correct route.

Path/drive/track/lane/road?

In this guide the word 'road' is used to denote anything from an unclassified road to a motorway: i.e. coloured yellow, brown, red/dark pink (or blue; if you are on one of these you are *lost*) on the Ordnance Survey map. A track is generally used to mean something less than a road, but wider than a path. It is likely to be unsurfaced unless it is a driveway to a farm or house. A lane is usually a bit more than a track but less than a road. Hence the hierarchy is: **path > track > lane > road**. Roughly.

Maps, descriptions, distances

While every effort has been made to maintain accuracy within the maps and descriptions in this guide, we have had to process a vast amount of information and we are unable to guarantee that every single detail is correct. Please exercise caution if a direction appears at odds with the route on the map. If in doubt, a comparison between the route, the description and a quick cross-reference with your map (along with a bit of common sense) should help ensure that you're on the right track. Note that distances have been measured off the map, and map distances rarely coincide 100 per cent with distances on the ground. Please treat stated distances as a guideline only.

Ordnance Survey maps are the most commonly used, are easy to read and many people are happy using them. If you're not familiar with OS maps and are unsure of what the symbols mean, you can download a free OS 1:25,000 map legend from **www.ordnancesurvey.co.uk**

Here are a few of the symbols and abbreviations we use on the maps and in our directions:

 ROUTE STARTING POINT

 ROUTE MARKER

 SHORTCUT

 OPTIONAL ROUTE

 ADDITIONAL GRID LINE NUMBERS TO AID NAVIGATION

PB = public bridleway
GR = grid reference
RHS/RH = Right-hand side/Right-hand
PF = public footpath
LHS/LH = Left-hand side/Left-hand

Abbreviations

In addition, the route descriptions can become long-winded so this book uses a number of extra abbreviations. These features were correct when the paths were walked but it must be remembered that stiles may become KGs and CGs are sometimes removed or filled in. All the walks have been followed at least twice while this book was in preparation, yet even over those few months features have changed in some places.

KG = Kissing gate
FB = Footbridge
CG = Cattle Grid
HG = Hunting gate (big enough for a horse but not a vehicle)
FG = Field gate (big enough for a tractor)
CW = Cotswold Way

Km/mile conversion chart

Metric to Imperial

1 kilometre [km]	1,000 m	0.6214 mile
1 metre [m]	100 cm	1.0936 yd
1 centimetre [cm]	10 mm	0.3937 in
1 millimetre [mm]		0.03937 in

Imperial to Metric

1 mile	1,760 yd	1.6093 km
1 yard [yd]	3 ft	0.9144 m
1 foot [ft]	12 in	0.3048 m
1 inch [in]		2.54 cm

M50
A40
A48
FOREST OF DEAN
Stonehouse
A419
M5
Dursley
19
16
Wotton-under-Edge
15
Thornbury
M5
20
M5
M4
A46
Yate
M4
17
Bristol
A46
18
A4
Bath

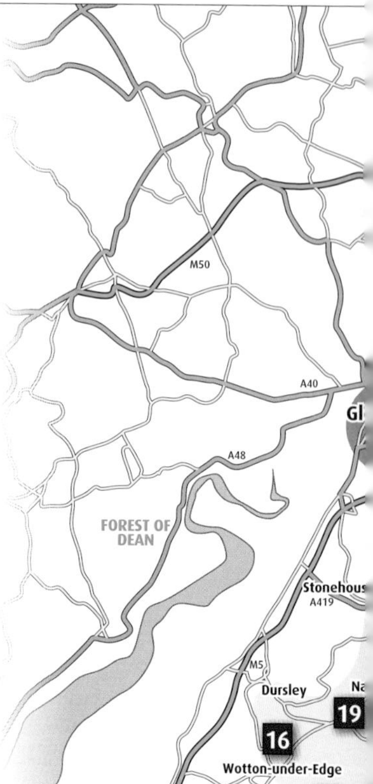

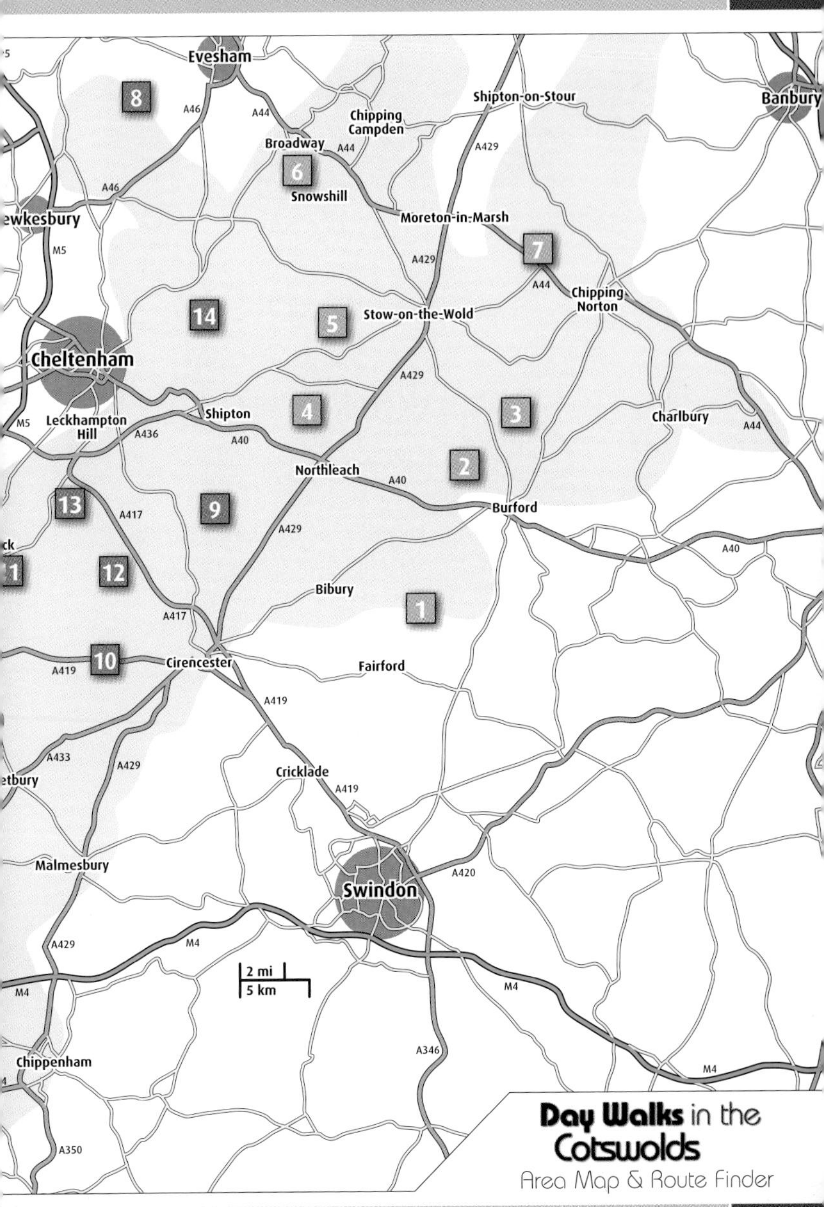
Evesham
Banbury
Shipton-on-Stour
Chipping Campden
Broadway
Snowshill
Moreton-in-Marsh
Chipping Norton
Stow-on-the-Wold
Cheltenham
Leckhampton Hill
Shipton
Northleach
Burford
Charlbury
Bibury
Cirencester
Fairford
Cricklade
Swindon
Malmesbury
Chippenham
2 mi
5 km
1
2
3
4
5
6
7
8
9
10
12
13
14
A46
A44
A429
A40
A436
A417
A419
A433
A420
A346
A350
M4
M5
Day Walks in the Cotswolds
Area Map & Route Finder

SECTION 1

The North-East Cotswolds

Extending into Oxfordshire, the north-east Cotswolds are less hilly than the west and south. The plateaux were – and still are – ideal for the siting of airstrips, and during the Second World War many small bases and relief landing grounds were established. The rivers Coln, Evenlode, Windrush, Churn and Leach all run south-east through the north-east Cotswolds, making their usually unhurried way to the Thames. The resulting water meadows make ideal summer grazing pastures, although changes in land use mean that in many places the land is now managed for hunting and shooting, with less livestock. Game cover is planted around field margins, where crops are grown – rape, corn and maize. This supports not just game birds, but deer – roe and muntjac – and small mammals which in turn support a large population of buzzards and, their territory moving westwards, the fork-tailed red kite.

THE RIVER LEACH IN EASTLEACH MARTIN (ROUTE 1)

THE CHURCH OF ST MARY THE VIRGIN, SALFORD (ROUTE 7)

THE RIVER LEACH, SOUTHROP

01 Southrop & the Eastleaches

11.5km/7.1miles

An easy and fairly flat walk which crosses and recrosses the River Leach in a journey between the villages of Southrop and Eastleach.

Southrop » ex-RLG Southrop » Eastleach Martin » Eastleach Turville » Leach Valley » Fyfield » Southrop

Start

On-street parking near school in Southrop. GR: SP 201035.

The Walk

This straightforward walk is located on a small spur of the Cotswolds north-east of Fairford, with its RAF base close by (expect passing military planes), and begins from the village of Southrop. After Southrop church the walk goes through a well-maintained courtyard bordered by the Tithe Barn and self-catering cottages, owned, like the village pub, by the Southrop Manor Estate, and marketed as 'Thyme'.

Leaving the village, a track and paths reveal the remains of RAF Southrop Relief Landing Ground (RLG), in use between 1940 and 1947. Intriguing broken brick walls and hardstandings remain under the brambles.

Field paths and tracks now lead to Eastleach. The church of St Michael and St Martin's, approached by a clapper bridge, is maintained by the Churches Conservation Trust. Eastleach is comprised of what were once two manors, Eastleach Martin to the east of the River Leach and Eastleach Turville to the west. Each manor had its own church.

The most famous curate of Eastleach Turville was John Keble, the Victorian church reformer who helped inspire the Oxford Movement. The clapper bridge across the Leach is named in his honour. Both churches date from the twelfth century; both are charming in different ways and both worth a visit.

A streamside walk is ahead, possibly boggy in places, then fields, and a quiet road around Fyfield hamlet, followed by a return to the River Leach just before arriving back in Southrop.

The walk does not directly pass the Victoria Inn but it is only a short distance from St Andrew's church, or the walker can divert and return to the village at one of the road crossings. Alternatively The Swan at Southrop is near the walk's end.

SOUTHROP & THE EASTLEACHES

DISTANCE: 11.5KM/7.1MILES » **TOTAL ASCENT:** 90M/275FT » **START GR:** SP 201035 » **TIME:** ALLOW 4.5 HOURS **MAP:** OS EXPLORER OL45, THE COTSWOLDS, 1:25,000 » **REFRESHMENTS:** VICTORIA INN, EASTLEACH TURVILLE; THE SWAN AT SOUTHROP » **NAVIGATION:** STRAIGHTFORWARD.

EASTLEACH MARTIN

01 SOUTHROP & THE EASTLEACHES

Directions – Southrop & the Eastleaches

S With school on left, walk slightly downhill to grass triangle on RHS. **Turn right**. At church, follow PF arrow **right** across gravelled area and through metal gate. **Left** around end of building and on reaching field look for KG in iron fence **half right**. Cross field **half right** aiming for ash tree on jutting-out corner, then **ahead** to gate. Continue along edge of builder's yard on to road; **turn right**. **Turn left** into Stonesfield Close and at end of fence/wall on right, **turn right**, with new houses behind wall on LHS. Follow path right, **angle left** then **ahead** to KG. Through (or over) FG on **right**, aim **half left** for pole and transformer in mid-field, then follow overhead line to exit field over fence on to track. **Turn right**.

2 (Water Tower shown on map (*Wr Twr*) is actually a pump house in opposite field, overgrown and hard to see so no use as a landmark.) Continue to road and **turn left.** At LH bend and junction, continue **straight ahead** on to track. Continue **half right** on to path to road at end.

3 **Turn right** then soon **right** signed *Public Footpath*. Cross the stream/ditch then keep to left hedge, after two fields passing to left of small, walled wood. **Straight ahead** past farm buildings to road. **Left** then **right** through HG. When field opens out, walk **half left** towards roofs, until HG in LH fence is visible. Down path; at track **right**; at road **left** then **right** past a row of cottages. **Left** towards war memorial, but keep **right** at junction. Take PF on **right** and cross River Leach by the clapper bridge known as 'Keble's Bridge'. Continue to church of St Michael and St Martin's.

4 Continuing through the churchyard, **turn left** at the road. At the junction the neighbouring church of St Andrew's, Eastleach Turville, with its saddleback tower, can be seen across the river. **Left** again to recross the Leach on the road bridge before turning **right** to the church of St Andrew's. After leaving the church, **keep right** then **turn right** immediately past Causey Barn cottage (which is almost opposite the path to Keble's Bridge, taken earlier). Up, and before cottage, **turn left** steeply up steps. **Turn right** at top. Continue along road to village hall **turning right** with hall on left; go through gate and **half left** in field to then follow left field boundary. Blue-topped fence posts at intervals mark this as a bridleway. Continue through fields until path drops to gated bridge over River Leach.

5 Cross FB, then keep to RH fence, crossing via a stile. Follow river, via further stiles and gates to remain in fields nearest water and follow well-defined track to road. At road **turn left** and **almost immediately right** up rough steps into woodland. Follow woodland path up then **turn right** and ahead out into field at end. Now keep to left hedge, to emerge on lane via footbridge at end of fields.

6 **Turn left** then **right** into field following path straight across to woods. Cross FB and continue **ahead** through wooded area and more fields to reach another road. **Turn left** then **keep right** at junction. At end of buildings **turn right** on to lane passing postbox (ignore earlier driveways without a postbox). **Continue ahead**, over stile into field then **half left** to gate and short track. Crossing the Leach again, **turn left** into field and another **half left** aiming for place in boundary where wall meets trees. Here there is a stile and a gate, and a well-marked path continues, emerging on to the main street of Southrop, between the school and the church.

ROLLING FARMLAND BY EASTLEACH MARTIN

THE CHURCH OF ST JOHN THE BAPTIST, GREAT RISSINGTON

02 The Windrush at Windrush

14.6km/9.1miles

Easy walking from Great Barrington to Great Rissington and a return alongside the River Windrush past the village of the same, Tolkienesque name.

Great Barrington » Great Rissington » Windrush » Little Barrington » Great Barrington

Start

On-street parking on main street in Great Barrington.
GR: SP 210137.

The Walk

From Great Barrington, well-signed paths cross fields to a country road, then after mingling with a flock of chickens, ducks and geese on a smallholding the walk goes through Great Rissington village, passing the Lamb Inn and the church before descending through fields to poplars growing on the banks of the meandering River Windrush. While home to heron and deer, the land is also managed for shooting partridge and pheasant, with field margins grown with game cover species, including sunflower, kale, millet and the purple-blue phacelia.

Detour away from the water past the sturdy buildings of Manor Farm, then back down to the grade II* listed Windrush Mill. Again leaving the river, continue on to Little Barrington, once home of the Strong family, master masons and suppliers of limestone. Limestone for the village was removed from the green area in the middle of the village, leaving the depression surrounded by cottages that is seen today.

Return via Barrington Mill to Great Barrington where another short circumnavigation of the village returns us to the start.

Barrington Park is visible across fields between Windrush and Little Barrington. The well-managed estate farms sheep, native cross-breed cattle and organic crops. On the edge, between the park and the village of Great Barrington, is the church of St Mary, not included on the walk but within easy distance for a visit if desired. A large, light airy space, it is known for having been desecrated by Thomas Wharton, 1st Marquess of Wharton and later member of parliament, during a drunken rampage in 1682.

THE WINDRUSH AT WINDRUSH

DISTANCE: 14.6KM/9.1MILES » **TOTAL ASCENT:** 160M/525FT » **START GR:** SP 210137 » **TIME:** ALLOW 4.5 HOURS **MAP:** OS EXPLORER OL45, THE COTSWOLDS, 1:25,000 » **REFRESHMENTS:** THE LAMB INN, GREAT RISSINGTON; THE FOX INN, GREAT BARRINGTON » **NAVIGATION:** STRAIGHTFORWARD.

LANE NEAR GREAT BARRINGTON

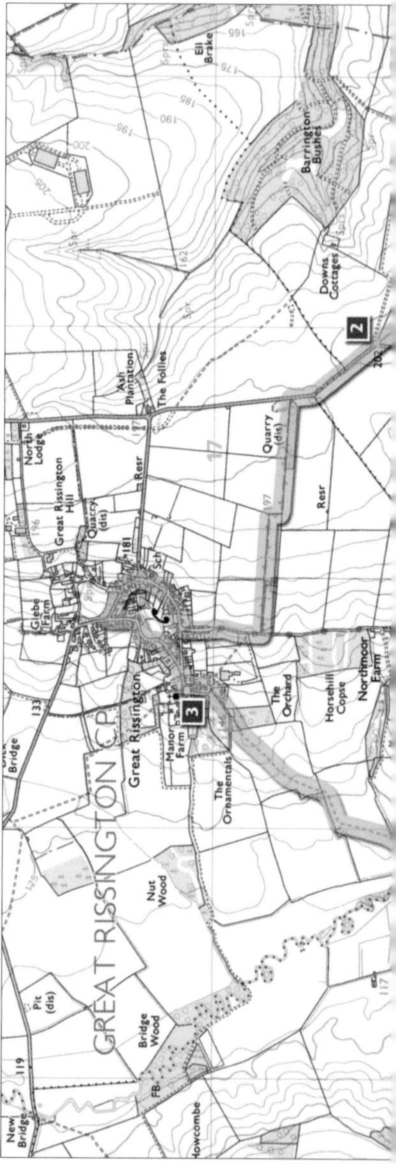

02 THE WINDRUSH AT WINDRUSH

Directions – The Windrush at Windrush

S Walk east away from the war memorial and with the telephone kiosk and postbox on your right. **Turn left** opposite The Old Smithy to end; **turn right** then into second field on left and **half right** to track. Follow track then fields ahead. Bridleway on map might go across centre of some fields, but clear signage asks walkers to use field perimeters. Continue about 2km to junction of paths in small copse/windbreak; **turn left**. Continue **straight ahead** to meet road at trig point.

2 **Turn right** at road junction. Meeting trees on left, take Restricted Byway **left** through trees then field. Through metal gate then follow RH boundary through smallholding passing sheds to join driveway. **Turn right** at end on to lane, continue to end, **turn right** at road. **Keep turning left** in village (**but ahead** at Orchard Bank) and **turn left** signed *Rectory Lane Only*. **Straight ahead** passing Blue Close Cottage and Orchard Cottage, and **bear right** at end of Rectory Lane. Church is on the right.

3 Route continues round to **left** past *Cotswold Meadows Private Road* sign; **fork right** after 50m, soon between conifer hedges, through HG, **bearing right** on lane. At end of trees follow sign **half left** down across field. Go through gateway/gap **right** then at arrow walk **half left** aiming for poplar trees in bottom corner of field.

4 Follow path through trees to the banks of the River Windrush, keeping the water on your right. Path meanders south through trees, through HG, over FB **keeping left** through scrub to field. **Ahead** across two fields then a **left** and **right** on to a track. **Ahead** on track past Manor Farm (worth a backward glance), then after about 500m follow arrows **right** at field boundary, crossing stream at bottom. Through gate then **left** to next FG. **Ahead** to jutting corner and through gate on **right**. Follow path around to bridge over Windrush just before Windrush Mill.

5 Cross mill driveway taking **RH** of two sets of steps, over stone stile. Follow fence to end of field, **bear right** and over another stone stile, dropping between walls to wide grassy track then lane to meet road; **bear left**. Follow road **left** with church on right and at end of cottages **turn right** through KG; walk **half left** to jutting corner then **ahead** on path across several fields.

6 To continue without visiting the Fox Inn, just stay **ahead** across fields for almost 1km in total, and then pass between stone barns. **Turn left** through gateway in wall, **then right** keeping village green (ex quarry, see page 11) on left. At junction **turn left** then **right** before telephone kiosk signed *To The Church*.

OR To visit the Fox Inn en route: in field with clump of trees continue to far boundary. Do not cross into next field but track **left** along hedge for one and a half sides of the field, then pass through gap **right** on to the road. The Fox is on the far side of the road, just around the bend. To continue the walk, **turn left** out of the pub and walk into the village, **turning left** after the telephone box and **ahead** to the church.

7 After the church **turn left** signed *No Through Road*. Follow road round to left and at end **turn right** over FB. Follow path **ahead** and around Barrington Mill over new bridges, then on meeting driveway stile **turn right** into field. Aim for large gable end with chimney (village hall) then join road through gate to **left** of hall. At road **turn right**, and **almost immediately turn left** between cottages to cut through to main road and return to the start.

FARMLAND FOOTPATH LEADING DOWN TO THE RIVER WINDRUSH

COCKSMOOR COPSE, BY BRUERN ABBEY

03 Bledington Morris

15.2km/9.4miles

Flat walking links three villages and a beautiful former abbey on the border of Oxfordshire and Gloucestershire.

Bruern » Fifield » Idbury » Foxholes Nature Reserve » Bould » Bledington » Bruern

Start

Roadside at small junction west of Bruern. GR: SP 260202. If it's dry or you have a 4WD it is also possible to park on the verge elsewhere along this stretch.

The Walk

'Bledington Morris' because a whole tradition of morris dance is named after the villages on this walk, although there has been no side (team) attached to the village of Bledington for many years. From the road, the walk crosses a field and picks up a track which skirts a private wood before leading through a broad scrubby area between hedges. At Fifield the route does a circuit of the village, which includes a path through the churchyard. Almost back at the end of the same track the route instead heads north, first between pony paddocks, then a newly planted wood – so new that it wasn't there when this walk was first planned. When mature, it will hide the alpacas grazing one field away. In and then out of Idbury village as field paths take the walk around the edge of the woods of the Foxholes Nature Reserve.

After the hamlet of Bould, fields and tracks reach Bledington, the largest village on the walk, and the walk passes St Leonard's church where a clerestory gives the interior a light, airy atmosphere. The King's Head Inn can provide refreshment. The route continues along the River Evenlode before crossing the Paddington to Hereford railway line. A couple more fields, then road the rest of the way, over the level crossing at Bruern.

An abbey stood here from 1147 to 1536, before a country house was constructed on the site in 1720 by the Cope family. Formerly a school, it became home to Michael Astor and his second wife Judy Innes. They moved to a 'cottage' in the grounds and after his death in 1980 the main house was sold. The stables and outhouses to the right of the road are now a complex of twelve top-range holiday cottages.

Note: This walk will be muddy after rain, as the Evenlode doesn't keep within its banks.

BLEDINGTON MORRIS

DISTANCE: 15.2KM/9.4MILES » **TOTAL ASCENT:** 145M/476FT » **START GR:** SP 260202 » **TIME:** ALLOW 4.5 HOURS **MAP:** OS EXPLORER OL45, THE COTSWOLDS, 1:25,000 » **REFRESHMENTS:** THE KING'S HEAD INN, BLEDINGTON » **NAVIGATION:** STRAIGHTFORWARD.

RIVER EVENLODE

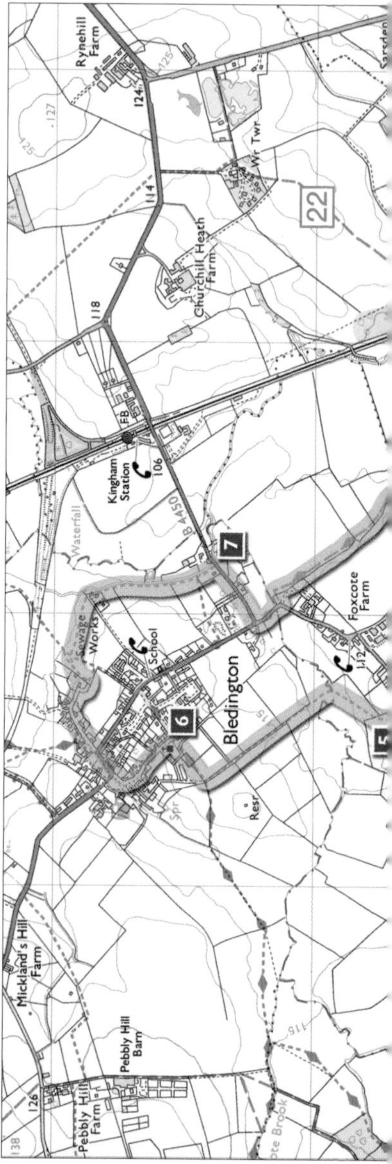

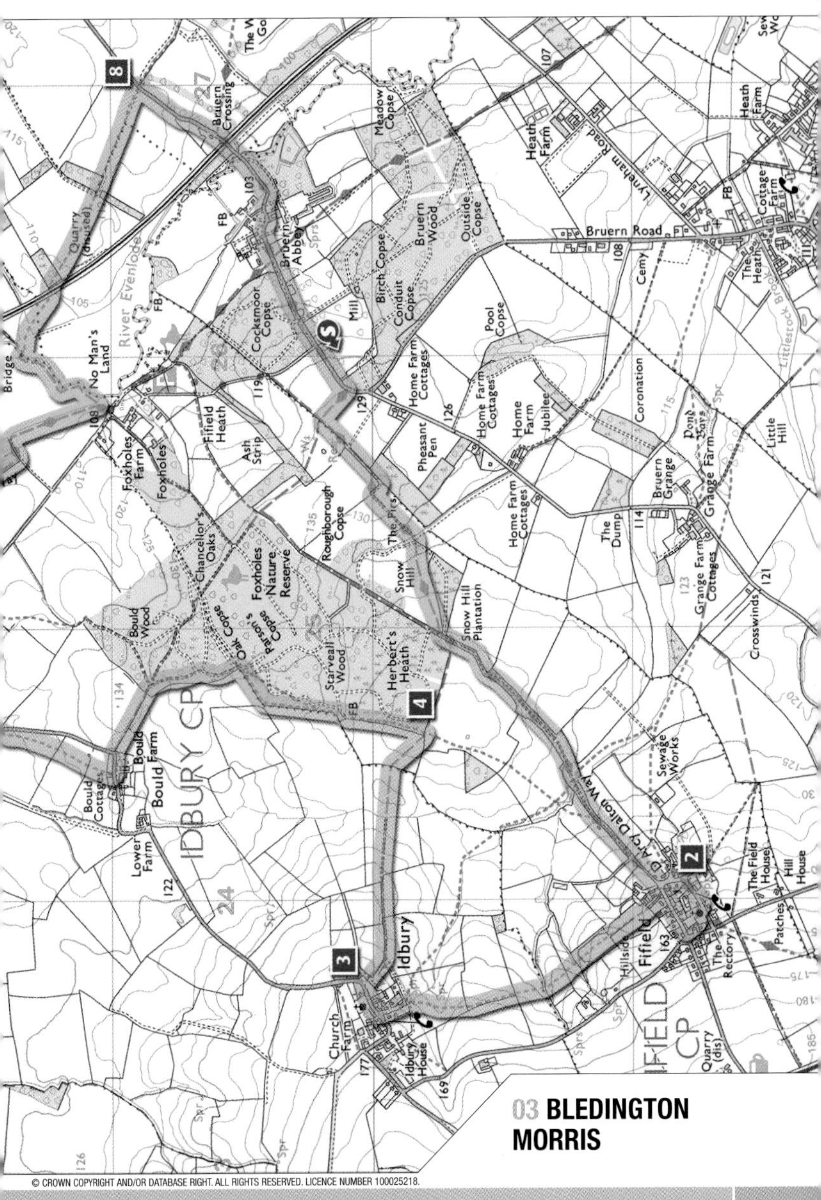

03 BLEDINGTON MORRIS

Directions – Bledington Morris

S Follow road **west** away from Bruern and with the No Through Road to the RHS. Approx. 200m after this junction and at a LH bend **turn right** into a field on D'Arcy Dalton Way. Walk straight across, then **left** keeping hedge on RHS. **Ahead**, changing to RHS of hedge on to track. Remain on track until private woodland then **bear right** along edge of wood then back on track ahead keeping on D'Arcy Dalton Way through broad tree-lined scrubby ride to road at Fifield village. **Turn left**.

2 Take the **first right**, then **right** into churchyard. Cross behind church towards far corner through KG and path back to road; **turn right**. Immediately after Pole Cottage, and almost back where you entered village, **turn left** on narrow PF soon opening on to track. Keep ahead across fields, two plank FBs and more fields. In the last field before Idbury village, walk **half right** initially towards church. Locate KG in boundary; **keep left** on track following through to the road, then **turn right** passing the church.

3 As road bends left, **turn right** through gate marked *Bridleway* apparently into horse yard. **Ahead** into field then **left**. Continue with hedge on LHS then **ahead** across two fields. At third field walk **half right** to corner of wood, pass through gap in hedge **right** then **hard left** to follow path inside wood, keeping wood edge on LHS.

4 Continue for about 1km, keeping to path closest to left wood boundary. **Ignore** the HG and footpath which leave the wood on the left but continue to a path junction where there is no continuation of the boundary path ahead. Now **turn left**, out of wood and into a field with hedge on LHS. **Turn left** at the road. After 70m **turn right** through a gate (PF sign may be half hidden in hedge) and **straight ahead** to FG then stile/FB and **ahead** again to road. **Turn left**. Before Foscot village sign, go **left** back into the same field (staying in field is an option, but this is not the PF).

5 **Half right** through gap and **half left** between fences to gate and FB. In field, **half left** to LHS of field corner to gate and on to a track running between hedges. **Ahead** to junction with gate ahead; **turn right**. Continue into churchyard, passing the church on your left.

6 **Turn left**, keeping church on LHS. At village green, follow road to **right** (unless visiting pub) and at next corner with the Old Post Office on your right, go **ahead** into No Through Road (Chapel Lane). Bending **right** to end then **right** on to track, **turn left** and **left** again to pass behind the house you just turned right in front of. Follow path **half right** to FB. **Do not cross** but, keeping river on left, continue to road by old mill.

7 **Turn right** (although, as the front of the mill is far more lovely than the back, a detour of a few metres to the left is worth it). At the right-hand bend **turn left** signed *Foscot & Idbury*. Leave road turning **left** at next right bend following *Oxfordshire Way Bridleway* signs and arrows. Be prepared for wet sections along track but continue **straight ahead** until emerging into field then follow with wood then ditch boundary on LHS to a bridge. **Walk left** over the bridge and **ahead** with stream to RHS, then cross gated bridge on the **right**. After bridge, **turn left**, then at next field **half right** crossing stream/ditch in mid-field and aim for wood at far side of railway crossing. **Stop, look and listen** then cross rails entering wood via HG. At field cross to gap in trees and continue in same line to gateway on to the road.

8 **Turn right** and follow the road over a level crossing, past Bruern Abbey and back to the start.

FIFIELD

ST BARTHOLOMEW'S CHURCH, NOTGROVE

04 Five Churches

15.6km/9.7miles

Easy navigation, clear tracks and very few steep sections help to make this a pleasant walk between the five churches and their associated settlements.

Notgrove » Salperton » Hazleton » Turkdean » Cold Aston » Notgrove

Start

Park in Notgrove opposite the telephone kiosk. This is the village hall car park and there is an honesty box for donations. GR: SP 108202.

The Walk

Leaving Notgrove, a downhill past kennels continues into the valley bottom before fields and track climb gently to Salperton, its tiny Norman church with macabre wall-painting standing right next to the main house of Salperton Park.

Again, fields and track sweep down then up, then down again into Hazleton – also spelled Haselton – with its twelfth-century church. A loop around the village passes a paddock where one may see a few Cotswold Lions, or at least rams of the Cotswold sheep breed. Continuing on, look for the ivy-covered doorway on the right.

Track and fields lead to the third village, finally reached by a ford and steep scramble up a bank: the name Turkdean meaning the 'valley of the boar'. On the inside wall of the church, also Norman era, a tale of woe describes how workmen washed a probably fourteenth-century wall-painting off the walls in 1967.

Then yet another clearly defined track continues to Cold Aston – also known as Aston Blank, the largest village on this route. Pub, manor house and, yes, another church. After leaving the village by road the route returns by the Gloucestershire Way through a long strip of woodland and across a field to the spired church at Notgrove and the start.

FIVE CHURCHES

DISTANCE: 15.6KM/9.7MILES » **TOTAL ASCENT:** 270M/886FT » **START GR:** SP 108202 » **TIME:** ALLOW 4.5 HOURS **MAP:** OS EXPLORER OL45, THE COTSWOLDS, 1:25,000 » **REFRESHMENTS:** THE PLOUGH INN AT COLD ASTON » **NAVIGATION:** STRAIGHTFORWARD.

Castle
New Covert
Quarry (disused)
Salperton
Limekiln Plantation
War Meml
Home Farm
227
232
Salperton Park
Cattle Grid
Poison Meadow
Gloucestershire Way
Farhill Covert
Salperton Park
254
2
Church Cover
Lamp Acre
Farhill Farm
Raspberry Brake
Long Walk
Diamond Way
Quarry (dis)
HAZLETON CP
Canon's Barn
223
Long Barrows
Coronation Copse
Rixon's Covert
H Ram
245 Hazleton Grove
Downs Barn
Lumley Covert
Quarry (Stone)
249
216
Milkwell Covert
Hazleton
3
Lower Barn
178
Shipton Downs Farm
Priory Farm
Resr
Thornborough Copse
217
Nut Tree Brake
The Downs Brake
Spring Wood
George Wood
Puesdown Inn
A 40
Hill Barn
227
241

04 FIVE CHURCHES

Directions – Five Churches

S With the telephone kiosk and Old Post Office on your right, walk south along the road to the junction. **Turn right** to the end of the road, **left** at the T-junction signed *Turkdean*, then **right** on to the lane marked *Public Bridleway*. After farm/kennels, go through gate and down field. After second gate and before reaching bottom of field, go through gate on **right**. Bear **half left** between ash tree and base of hill, down to gate/FB in lower field boundary. Walk straight up field valley, and **bear slight right** at end on to track. Continue **straight ahead** for 1.5km to CG. To visit Salperton church (N° 1), cross the CG then **sharp right**.

2 Return to recross CG, now turning **right**. Continue through gate on to track **straight ahead** into valley. Pass through HG **ahead** with wood to left. Stay **ahead** at buildings to road then walk **straight ahead**, downhill, with church (N° 2) on left.

3 Continue on road down the hill then back up the other side. **Turn right** into side road after Hillside Cottage. Follow road to end and **turn left**. Keep **straight ahead**, later marked *Unsuitable for Motors* to farm where road becomes a stoned, sometimes-muddy track (Sabrina Way). After 1km track ends. Continue **straight ahead** through gate then round to **right**, along valley bottom. Pick up track and climb to gateway. Through gate on **right**, then **half left** down field to a gate and stone slab bridge. **Half left** again on to grassy track and **ahead** to gate. **Turn left** over/through a ford, pass cottage and continue straight up steep, stony PF to road. **Turn left** into Turkdean. Church (N° 3) is on the right.

4 Continue around LH bend then **turn right** at large grass triangle signed *Restricted Byway, Macmillan Way* and *Sabrina Way*. Continue on this track for 2.8km, by which time it has become a road. At a LH bend and before house on RHS go **right** over stone stile. Keep to left boundary into second field then **half right** to gate. **Turn left** on road into Cold Aston (Aston Blank). Plough Inn is on LHS. Continue round to left, signed *Notgrove*, deviating to the church (N° 4) on the right, adjacent to the primary school, if desired.

5 Keep **ahead** out of the village for approx. 700m passing national speed limit signs to beech windbreak. **Turn left** on path through trees, signed *Gloucestershire Way/Public Bridleway*, to driveway at end. **Turn right** and through first gate **left**. Continue down to trees in very bottom and middle of field then **ahead** up the other side and through gate to **right** of cottages. Another very short deviation **left** leads to Notgrove church (N° 5). Returning, keep to LH road, passing barn with pigeon loft. Look for HG on **right** with path across small field which cuts a corner, then **right** a few metres back to the start.

TURKDEAN

THE RIVER EYE MEANDERING THROUGH LOWER SLAUGHTER

05 Naunton & the Slaughters

17.2km/10.7miles

Choose your own rate of progress through touristy Bourton-on-the-Water and Lower Slaughter, with gently undulating off-road walking through fields and woodland.

Naunton » River Windrush » Bourton-on-the-Water » River Eye » Lower Slaughter » Upper Slaughter » Naunton

Start

Roadside in Naunton.
GR: SP 115234.

The Walk

Before leaving Naunton there is a seventeenth-century dovecote to explore – or save it for later as the walk returns this way. After a low ridge the walk picks up the valley of the River Windrush, then at Lower Harford goes through the hidden remains of a medieval village. Traditional longhorn cattle and Cotswold sheep live here, as well as, in season, a profusion of wild flowers including dropwort and yellow-wort, as well as quaking grass, in the species-rich grassland. Now a gentle climb into woods, almost reaching the disused line of Great Western's Banbury and Cheltenham Direct Railway (1881–1964) before walking through Aston Farm and crossing the Windrush at the mill. After a small but outstanding Cotswold cottage garden decide whether to use the Macmillan Way to walk direct to Lower Slaughter (which shortens the walk to 14.5km/9miles), or instead continue to Bourton-on-the-Water with its ducks, shops and selfie-sticks.

If visiting Bourton, the walk continues to follow the Windrush, crossing the main Fosse Way, then uses a delightful bridge and back lanes to reach the main street. Pass through the churchyard and, after recrossing the Fosse, fields lead to Lower Slaughter.

Lower Slaughter also gets its fair share of tourists, but following the River Eye to Upper Slaughter (one of the country's few 'Doubly Thankful' villages, having lost no one in either the first or second world wars) the crowds will have gone, and the walk continues with five kilometres of quiet fields and tracks back to Naunton where another streamside stretch arrives by the clapper bridge by the dovecote. There is a bit of climbing en route, but for the fit walker these are gentle undulations rather than hills.

NAUNTON & THE SLAUGHTERS

DISTANCE: 17.2KM/10.7MILES » **TOTAL ASCENT:** 203M/666FT » **START GR:** SP 115234 » **TIME:** ALLOW 5 HOURS
MAP: OS EXPLORER OL45, THE COTSWOLDS, 1:25,000 » **REFRESHMENTS:** THE BLACK HORSE INN, NAUNTON; BOURTON SHOPS & RESTAURANTS; THE SLAUGHTERS COUNTRY INN AND THE OLD MILL (BOTH LOWER SLAUGHTER) » **NAVIGATION:** STRAIGHTFORWARD.

Quarry (Limestone)
Summerhill
Quarry (disused)
Tumulus
Grange Hill Farm
Warden's Way
Brockhill Farm
6
Eyford Knoll
Tumulus
Resr
Parker's Barn
Hill Barn
Brockhill Quarry (Limestone)
Wales Barn
The Brake
B 4068
Naunton
Waterloo Farm
Pit (dis)
Brockhill Barn
CH
MS
Sewage Works
Harford Bridge
Naunton Downs Golf Club
Harfordhill Farm
Lodge's Barn
Lower Harford Farm
Ford
Hill Farm
2
Quarry (disused)
Medieval Village of Lower Harford (site of)
Roundhill Farm
River Windrush
202
Roundhill Fox Covert
Bowman's Hay
Upper Harford
Airstrip
21
216
Windrush Farm
201
237
Tumulus
Coldmoor Coppice
Folly Farm
Camp Farm
Pemmington Coppice
Belham's Gore
The Buckleap
New Barn
Gloucestershire Way
Claylodge Coppice
223
Quarry (disused)

© CROWN COPYRIGHT AND/OR DATABASE RIGHT. ALL RIGHTS RESERVED. LICENCE NUMBER 100025218.

05 NAUNTON & THE SLAUGHTERS

Directions – Naunton & the Slaughters

S Locate the telephone kiosk close to the brow and start to walk downhill (east) with telephone kiosk on left. **Turn right** into No Through Road marked *Naunton Dovecote* and *Warden's Way*. Follow Warden's Way sign past dovecote through gate then **straight ahead** up bank to road. Cross and continue **straight ahead** on PB alongside golf course, dropping into field, **slightly left** then down track; cross River Windrush and **turn left** through gate.

2 Now through three fields following line of telegraph poles. In third field the path correctly climbs to top-right corner but lower gate is clearly used too and route (Windrush Way) continues after road crossing opposite this lower gate. Again, across several fields with River Windrush to the left. Path then climbs into woods (arrow on post), crosses one field with hedge to left and back into woodland. After meeting disused railway embankment and bridge, leave woodland across field to Aston Farm. Walk through farmyard between buildings, along short farm drive to road, then **turn left**.

3 Cross River Windrush then walk past cottage on left with glorious garden on right. Continue on to track.* Continue on path round to **right** following Windrush Way for 1km to the A429. Cross with care into Lansdowne. After 250m take PF **right**, crossing river on stone FB. Continue to road then **straight ahead** and to the **right** into Bow Lane. **Turn left** at the end, following road to High Street, and **turn left**. Continue to church and **turn right** into church driveway. **Straight ahead** at end, passing schools, to Station Road; **turn left**. Cross A429 at crossing, **turn right**, then **left** on to Heart of England Way. Where main path bends right, follow narrow grassy muddy path to LHS of narrow triangular field; cross FB at end. Aiming for second electricity pole, then stile, continue in same direction **half right**, over stile on to lane. **Turn right**.

SC ***SC**: To omit Bourton-on-the-Water, look for fingerpost, **turn left** on to woodland path signed *Gloucestershire Way/Public Bridleway*. In second field go through HG on **right** and cross field diagonally towards clump of trees to another HG. Cross road on to PB. Continue **straight ahead** to next road and ahead downhill on road opposite.

4 For both routes: continue to end; **slight left** to cross Windrush on FB into Lower Slaughter. **Turn right** and at junction where Windrush crosses under road **turn left** and **keep left**, passing church. Continue round left bend but at right bend go **ahead** through KG, signed *Upper Slaughter* and *Public Footpath*. After several KGs and HGs, **bear half left** in field to join Warden's Way through gate; **turn right**.

5 **Straight ahead** across fields with River Eye to left. **Sharp left** over stone FB, continue to road, **turn left**. Follow bend **right** then **right** at junction/triangle to pass telephone kiosk, towards a ford. Before dropping to ford, **turn left** on to track signed *Warden's Way*. Continue on obvious path signed (usually) *Warden's Way* across fields and on woodland tracks to road. **Turn left**, passing parkland. At the end of the park is a lane and, immediately after, a track, both on **right**: take the track passing close to cottages then through FG. Again, follow obvious path up and across fields to a barn. **Turn left** after barn to road.

6 Cross road into field via HG. Keep alongside road against right hedge, fence or wall across several fields and driveways until *Warden's Way* sign **left** on to track, continuing **straight ahead** on to path downhill where track bends left. Path bends **right** then climbs into field. **Half right** across three fields, then downhill through belt of trees. Follow track across and down field to road. **Turn left**. At T-junction (note Black Horse Inn on left) go **ahead** passing to RHS of The Old Band Room. Cross river then immediately **turn right** over stone stile on to streamside path which emerges from trees at gate close to the dovecote. **Turn right** back up to the road and the start.

FARMLAND OUTSIDE BOURTON-ON-THE-WATER

BROADWAY TOWER

06 Broadway & Snowshill

18.1km/11.2miles

Two of the Cotswold's most popular villages, a couple of relatively stiff climbs, and views across the Vale of Evesham to the Malvern Hills.

St Eadburgha's Church » Broadway Tower » Broadway » Buckland » Laverton » Laverton Hill » Snowshill » St Eadburgha's Church

Start

By St Eadburgha's church, 1km south of Broadway. GR: SP 097363.

The Walk

Start a kilometre out of Broadway, away from the coaches and the visitors all of whom miss the church of St Eadburgha. A steady climb up a track leads to the Broadway Tower Country Park where you can pay to visit the nuclear bunker and the tower which stands at the second-highest point in the Cotswolds, or continue downhill again following the Cotswold Way across fields to Broadway village.

Dodge the tourists along the main street then turn left and leave them all behind. The footpath becomes a bit muddy and vague through Broadway Coppice, after which a few wonky stiles have to be negotiated before the village of Buckland, located along a No Through Road so free from passing traffic. The church of St Michael is still full of treasures despite the theft of a sixteenth-century book in 2012.

There is a good, surfaced path to Laverton where a long track climbs through sheep-grazed grassland before joining, then leaving, the Cotswold Way and crossing farmland to drop into Snowshill. The sixteenth-century manor (National Trust) is a nice-enough house, but is best known for the eclectic collections of former owner Charles Wade. At the church you are told picnicking in the churchyard is prohibited – unlike at other places in the Cotswolds which are far more welcoming.

Drop through fields to the valley bottom, and then back up through woods and fields to meet a track. After going through the middle of a farmyard a zigzag of field boundaries leads back to St Eadburgha's Church (named for the great-granddaughter of Alfred the Great) at the start.

BROADWAY & SNOWSHILL

DISTANCE: 18.1KM/11.2MILES » **TOTAL ASCENT:** 185M/607FT » **START GR:** SP 097363 » **TIME:** ALLOW 5.5–6.5 HOURS **MAP:** OS EXPLORER OL45, THE COTSWOLDS, 1:25,000 » **REFRESHMENTS:** SNOWSHILL ARMS, SNOWSHILL; VARIOUS IN BROADWAY » **NAVIGATION:** MOSTLY STRAIGHTFORWARD; SOME CARE NEEDED IN BUCKLAND WOOD.

CONEYGREE LANE

06 BROADWAY & SNOWSHILL

Directions – Broadway & Snowshill

S Walk uphill on a wide, stony track opposite St Eadburgha's Church, signed *Public Footpath to Broadway Tower*, for approx. 1km. At the end **turn right**, through gate then **half left** towards bungalow, picking up a track. At wood boundary **turn left** through FG then **straight ahead**, climbing. After buildings **turn left** through HG (*Public Footpath* and *Cotswold Way Circular Walk* signs). **Track half right** to LHS of shop/cafe and, **before** reaching public road, **turn left** through gate in high fence, signed *Broadway Tower* and *Nuclear Bunker.*

2 Passing the tower, meet track (Cotswold Way). **Turn left** on to broad track then fields, keeping downhill and following arrows on posts to later bend round **right** and emerge in Broadway. **Turn left.** Fight your way smugly past day trippers to **turn left** into Church Street (Cotswold Way). Pass church and at end of church wall **turn right.** Keep to RH fence in field and continue, crossing next field to road. Cross road, but **do not** take Cotswold Way; instead follow signs over stile **half right** signed *Footpath to Buckland.* While climbing second stile, look ahead to stile into wood and aim for this across field.

3 Entering wood by left-hand stile, go **ahead** crossing track and staying close to bottom edge of wood, **bearing right** to follow direction of arrow nailed to tree stump, after which correct path becomes muddy but more distinct. Continue, emerging on to bottom of steep field. Follow path round to **right**, contouring to lower margin of trees. At fork and remains of a stile, **keep left**, following line of wood, then **ahead** over a couple of sloping stiles (which may get replaced) then **right** and down to stable yard, walking in front of stables to road. **Turn right.**

4 Pass or visit Buckland church then continue past telephone kiosk and postbox, looking for sign **left** on to *Public Bridlepath, Winchcombe Way.* **Ahead** on this good, surfaced path to Laverton. At road **turn left** (marked dead end) and at end continue on to *Restricted Byway/Winchcombe Way*, climbing steeply on well-defined track for well over 1km to gate on to Cotswold Way. Take Cotswold Way **right**, joining driveway and still climbing. **Keep ahead** where Cotswold Way turns back right at CG to Shenberrow Farm. After 70m **turn right** on to Restricted Byway; now keep **straight ahead** along field boundaries for almost 1km to fingerpost, then **turn ¾ left** back across and down fields to road. **Turn right. Ahead** past a lane end to road junction. **Turn left** downhill into Snowshill village.

5 Passing church, pub and manor **continue** on road to entrance to main National Trust car park (just before national speed limit sign) on left, signed *Snowshill Manor*, and take KG **left** into field, following path downhill and round to left then into wood and over stream. Climb round to **right** through woods then look for a gate on the **left** into a field. Go **ahead**, climbing and keeping near LH fence into trees; follow path to track and **turn right**. (NB If you miss the gate left and find yourself clambering up into field over a bank and landslip, make your way one field to the left.)

6 Stay on track through gate, and remain on track to drop to a farm, passing through the farmyard. Exiting yard, take path **right** between fence and hedge/barn. Continue to later **zigzag left**, **right**, **left**, **right downhill** following LH fence with view of St Eadburgha's Church in valley. Continue **ahead** to road. **Turn left** and return to the start.

BROADWAY

KING'S MEN STONE CIRCLE

07 Rollright & Adlestrop

20.2km/12.6miles

A fairly easy if long walk incorporating the Neolithic and the Iron Age with the wealth that was and is living in the area and shaping the landscape.

A44 » Rollright Stones » Little Rollright » Salford » Cornwell » Daylesford » Adlestrop » Chastleton » A44

Start

Lay-by on A44 just north of the Greedy Goose pub and the junction with the A436. GR: SP 269289.

The Walk

This route takes the walker from Gloucestershire into Warwickshire and Oxfordshire, and following field boundaries near the top of a ridge, there is a real feel of the wolds for which the Cotswolds are named. A road section drops to the private hamlet of Little Rollright – permissive paths secure the residents' privacy, though the public footpaths through the middle remain open – before the steady climb to the Rollright Stones: pass the Whispering Knights to reach the King's Men stone circle, while the King is on his own in a field across the road. (Small charge, if you can find the honesty box.)

Returning to Little Rollright by the same route, cross fields to the village of Salford. In autumn, a basket of apples on a wall bore the label, *Windfalls, please help yourself (mind the wasps!)*, and trees overhanging the churchyard drop walnuts for walkers and squirrels. Cross the A44 and continue to another privately owned hamlet, Cornwell Manor. The tiny church is separate and open. On again through field and wood to Daylesford hill farm and stud, owned by the Bamford family of JCB fame. The path goes right through the immaculate yard, but everyone encountered has been welcoming.

After park and woodland reach Adlestrop, the former rectory visited by Jane Austen and thought to be the inspiration for *Mansfield Park*. The village is better known for Edward Thomas's poem, reproduced in the bus shelter. The walk passes a small, thatched post office store with irregular opening hours (cups of tea and ice creams, when open).

After a damp valley bottom, fields climb to Chastleton House (National Trust) before a short diversion to an Iron Age hill fort, Chastleton Barrow. There is little to be seen except an earth bank topped by mature trees but it would be a shame to miss it. An open country lane with views across the countryside leads back to the start.

ROLLRIGHT & ADLESTROP

DISTANCE: 20.2KM/12.6MILES » **TOTAL ASCENT:** 330M/1,083FT » **START GR:** SP 269289 » **TIME:** ALLOW 6.5 HOURS **MAP:** OS EXPLORER OL45, THE COTSWOLDS, 1:25,000 » **REFRESHMENTS:** GREEDY GOOSE AT A44/A436; ADLESTROP PO; CHASTLETON HOUSE » **NAVIGATION:** STRAIGHTFORWARD.

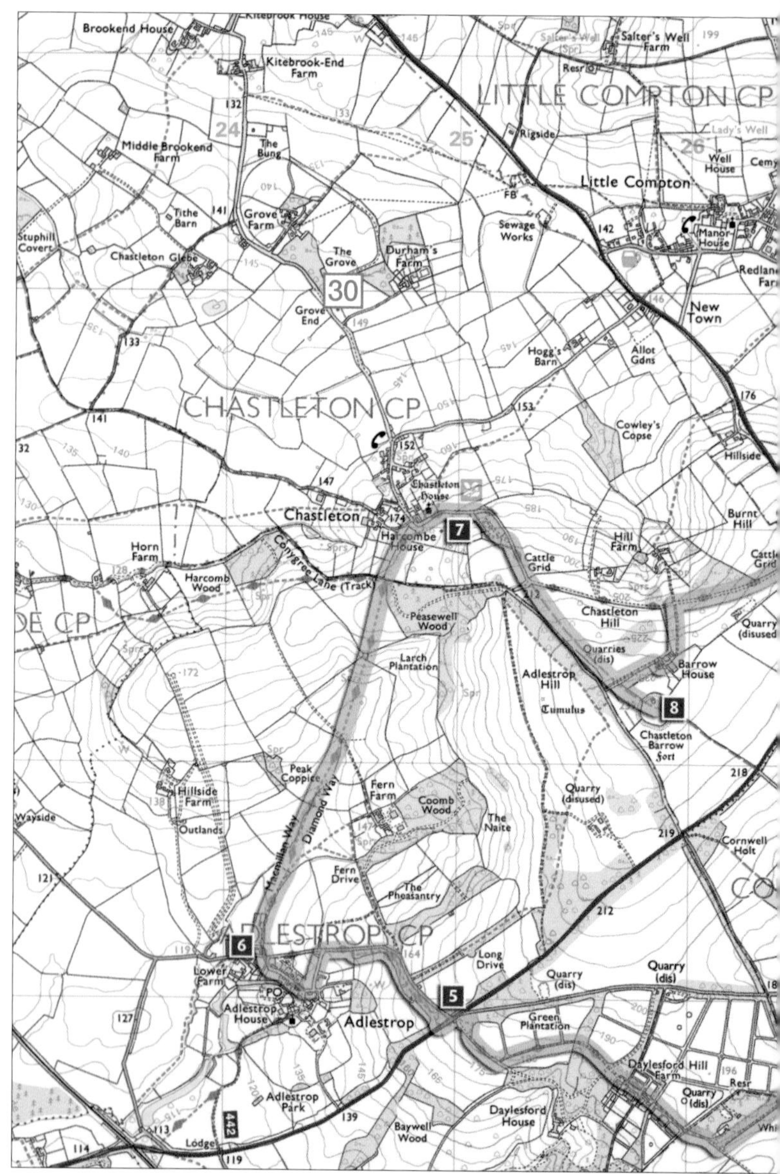

Neakings
Farm
Hydraulic Rams
Rollright Stones
King Stone
Turnpikehill Barn
Kings Men Stone Circle
Whispering Knights Burial Chamber
3
216
Slade Farm
Quarries (dis)
27
28
29
30
Oakham
Baker's Hill
Little Rollright
2
Moat
Windmill Farm
Pond Bay
Fish Pond
Manor Farm
148
238
Twin Brook Farm
247
Pump House
Quarry (disused)
243
D'Arcy Dalton Way
Shakespeare's Way
Quarry (disused)
239
Hirons Hill Farm
216
Quarry (dis)
Quarries (disused)
FB
143
MS
Quarry (dis)
226
Quarry (dis)
Springhill Farm
198
214
Rectory Farm
Hollis Hill Farm
SALFORD CP
FB
Rushy Bottom
Greathouse Barn
Larches Farm
164
Fisher's Barn
Cross (rems of)
Salford
182
Cross (rems of)
141
Park Farm
Sewage Works
Harkaway House
184
Salford Mill
Shakespeare's Way
131
127
Glebe Farm
Bridge Field
Cornwell Manor
4
Nuholme
172
Quarry (dis)
Reservoir
Filter Bed
143
Mill Copse
Cornwell Hill Farm
123
Swailsford Bridge
Kingham Hill School
Hill Farm
07 ROLLRIGHT & ADLESTROP

Directions – Rollright & Adlestrop

S With the lay-by on your left, walk **north** along verge for approx. 200m and take first lane on **right** marked *Macmillan Way*. Pass farm and continue **ahead** on track and path along field boundaries for almost 2km to a road. **Turn right**. Continue for 1.25km to end and cross on to track keeping downhill, later along new beech avenue into Little Rollright.

2 At church follow permissive path **left**, looking out for sign for D'Arcy Dalton Way and path **left*** to Rollright Stones. Follow path uphill, cross road on to track and ahead across two fields. Whispering Knights burial chamber comes into view behind railings ahead and left. At field/wood boundary **turn left** uphill to Whispering Knights. Continue to top of field and **turn left** to the King's Men stone circle. The King Stone is across the road.

3 Retrace your steps. In Little Rollright (at *) continue between hedges on D'Arcy Dalton Way, climbing out of Little Rollright on well-marked path across fields and woodland. After stile and stream the path goes through FG on **right** then continues **left** into woods. Emerging into field, follow **left** boundary, over two stiles then **half left** diagonally across field, aiming for stile to **right** of far corner. **Turn left** on track then **right** at road and **left** between wall and hedge signed *Public Footpath*. At end **turn right**, passing play area on left and **turn right** into The Leys. As road bends right, take stile **left** into field, signed *D'Arcy Dalton Way*. Follow round **left**, and the church comes into view. Continue across field and, passing with block wall on left, stile in far corner leads into churchyard.

Leaving by main churchyard gate, **ahead** on narrow path between hedge left and fence right to main A44. **Turn right** and cross opposite *50 mph* sign on to a path marked *Bridleway Cornwell* and *D'Arcy Dalton Way*. Continue on obvious track to Glebe Farm where path goes **half left** between barns, then down farm drive to lane. **Turn right** then after about 20m **left** into field. Walk downhill to cross muddy ditch/stream on concrete bridge; **keep left** up the other side and the east end of Cornwell Church can be seen.

4 Continue along church path towards Cornwell Manor. Follow sign **half right** across field to KG on to driveway. Path then continues parallel to driveway, through orchard. At lane, **turn left** towards buildings then follow bend right **turning left** at road,

continuing to T-junction. **Turn left** signed *Chipping Norton.* Opposite manor entrance climb bank on **right** and in field follow arrow **half right** to gate/stile (**NOT** D'Arcy Dalton Way and **NOT** the hunting gate close to the RH hedge). On track, go **ahead** through farmyard and continue into fields. Cross road and on into woods on far side. At end **turn right** on to well-maintained track/road with signs warning of farm vehicles and requests to keep off verges. Follow past fenced paddocks to buildings and follow arrow **ahead** through gravel yard, leaving via black-painted gates, then **straight ahead** on track over bridge and past horse paddocks. **Turn right** where track meets main driveway. **Ahead** to the end, with a short **right-and-left diversion** to avoid a private lodge.

5 **Turn left** at road. Walk past the junction and after a few metres cross into the woods and follow the path parallel to the Adlestrop road. Continue until a stile exits the woods. **Turn left** and then **left** at first road junction to drop into Adlestrop. **Continue ahead** following road round to right to the post office with its circular, thatched roof. Continue **straight ahead**, keeping the post office on your left.

6 At road end glance right to the old station sign in the bus stop, before continuing **ahead** on to track then over stile at gate, following signs/arrows for Macmillan Way. **Half left** across field to stile in far left corner. Over stile in fence on **left**, then **right** and keep along bottom of field. After next stile go diagonally up across middle of field to gate and stile into trees in top corner. Follow Macmillan Way arrow **half right** across next field and through lime avenue with Chastleton House ahead. **Turn right** on road to pass front of house.

7 Cross into the dovecote field opposite the house and follow path **left** to the NT car park. Leave by the vehicular entrance and **turn right**. At bend and NT *Exit Traffic* sign, **turn left** through gate adjoining CG and **immediately right** through HG into field. Continue along length of field parallel to right field boundary to farm driveway. Cross, go through LH gate and **ahead** to Chastleton Barrow.

8 **Return** to farm driveway and **turn right** towards buildings. Passing gate to house on right, go **right** through second gateway and then **left**, through yard and on to track **left** and downhill to the road. **Turn right** and follow road back to A44 opposite where the route left it at the start of the walk. **Turn right** for 200m to return to the lay-by.

SECTION 2

The North-West Cotswolds

Further west the Cotswolds become more hilly, with streams flowing westwards past many disused or converted mills, once part of the thriving woollen industry. This is Laurie Lee country, though the simple stone weavers' cottages have mostly been extended to house families whose employment is in Cheltenham or Gloucester. From the tops of the hills, or the Cotswold Edge, there are views to the Malverns and over the Severn plain.

BARROW WAKE, BIRDLIP (ROUTE 13)

LOOKING ACROSS TO SWIFT'S HILL FROM FURNERS FARM (ROUTE 11)

ST MARY THE VIRGIN, ELMLEY CASTLE

08 Bredon Hill

12.9km/8miles

Far-reaching views from the steep slopes of Bredon Hill across the River Avon to the Malverns and beyond.

Elmley Castle » Great Comberton » Bredon Hill » Elmley Castle

Start

Elmley Castle picnic site, on the road at south-east approach to the village.
GR: SO 984410.

The Walk

Bredon Hill is on a north-western spur of the Cotswolds AONB, protruding into Worcestershire, and Elmley Castle is typical of the region; a black-and-white, half-timbered village. From the tiny picnic site the road into the village passes through a pinch point for drivers, with buildings less than three metres apart.

Footpath then bridlepath leads through flat farmland around the base of the hill. The Regency-style house across fields on the right is Bricklehampton Hall: built in 1848 it is now a nursing home. Walk through the churchyard at Great Comberton almost on the banks of the River Avon before joining the Wychavon Way. After a steady climb, a flatter section leads to Woollas Hall, built in 1611 and just visible through trees. Turning back uphill just before the hall cottages the route now continues to the top of Bredon Hill (299 metres) where the mid-eighteenth-century Parsons' Folly (or Banbury Stone Tower) is now a siting for mobile phone masts, rather than the summer house that was intended. From here there are views down to the meanders of the River Avon and across to the Malvern Hills. A topograph is set into a flat stone a bit beyond the tower.

After following the top of the hill for over two kilometres the route drops through woodland with the remains of eleventh-century Elmley Castle hill fort on the left. After a steep, marshy field the gradient becomes less severe, and an easy stroll across two fields returns to Elmley Castle via the churchyard to the Queen Elizabeth inn and restaurant, with coffee and cake available as well as normal pub fare.

BREDON HILL

DISTANCE: 12.9KM/8MILES » **TOTAL ASCENT:** 315M/1,033FT » **START GR:** SO 984410 » **TIME:** ALLOW 4 HOURS **MAP:** OS EXPLORER 190, MALVERN HILLS & BREDON HILL, 1:25,000 » **REFRESHMENTS:** QUEEN ELIZABETH INN, ELMLEY CASTLE » **NAVIGATION:** STRAIGHTFORWARD.

ST MICHAEL'S, GREAT COMBERTON

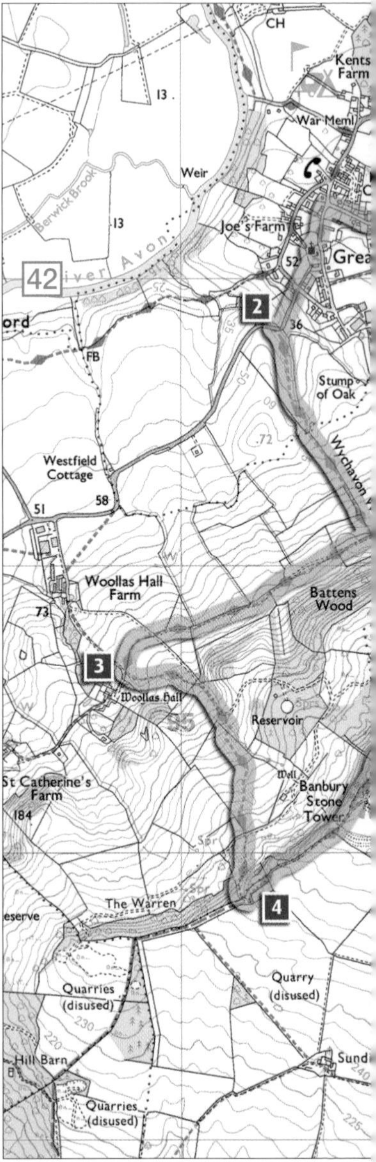

08 BREDON HILL

Directions – Bredon Hill

S Leaving picnic site on LHS continue into village through narrow pinch point. **Turn left** then **right** into Hill Lane. At sharp left corner, follow PF fingerpost **right. Turn left** through two HGs into yard. **Straight ahead** across yard to three FGs then stile in **right** fence. (There is also a permissive path to the Combertons which bypasses the farmyard. Either route will do.) Continue **half left** diagonally across to bottom left of field. Cross stile and **left**. Now **continue ahead** across fields until a KG meets a track. **Turn right** on to PB. **Ignore** first PF on left and **continue ahead** for almost 300m; **turn left** on to PB signed *Great Comberton* (though you may have to look back to read the sign). **Ahead** again over fields and tracks until track becomes a lane becomes a road. **Continue ahead**. At T-junction **turn left**, and then **right** into churchyard. At western (tower) end of church **take right fork** on grassy path to KG passing to right of Church Cottage. Follow enclosed lane to road junction, then **left/ahead** down 11% hill.

2 At RH bend, **turn left** on to PF signed *Wychavon Way*. Climbing, keep near to stream on left then up through gate. Well-marked Wychavon Way continues to climb, then turns **right** and meets a track. Remain on track to cross driveway next to a CG, then **ahead** across field with fence to LHS to Woollas Hall.

3 Climb stile on **left** into field before the cottages. Walk **half left** to climb the field to remeet driveway crossed previously. Now walk up track until it bends left and is marked *Private*. Take PF **right**, after gate climbing steeply **half left** to marker post, seat and further marker posts. After gate, take sunken path, then gate into woods, **turning left** through beech woods at junction where ground levels.

4 Keeping to LH wall, **continue ahead** to Banbury Stone Tower, then continue around top of Bredon Hill still keeping to LH wall. At FG by copse ahead, go through gate, still on Wychavon Way. Follow sign for Wyche Way, maintaining height and keeping fence to RHS to meet top corner of wood. Continue along upper edge of wood, fenced on both sides.

5 At the wooden seat, **turn left** into woods and steeply down, entering field after about 500m. At first keep to left then looking for marker post **bear right** over a wooden bridge. **Turn left** and continue descending over another bridge to the boundary; at gate marked *Private* **turn left**, keeping fence now to RHS. **Ahead** through gate on to track, then **immediately left** over another bridge and through gate into field. **Half right** across field to stile. In this next field the path is unclear; it should go ahead across field then **left** on meeting a right-to-left path which leaves field just to left of small ash tree (and left of red-brick house). If in doubt, follow field boundary left. Leave field between pony paddocks and **ahead** into churchyard. Leaving by main gate, the Queen Elizabeth (seating outside at rear; dogs welcome in bar) is just ahead on left for well-earned refreshment, or **turn right** through pinch point to car and picnic area.

THE RIVER AVON, BY GREAT COMBERTON

RESTRICTED BYWAY ABOVE CHEDWORTH

09 Chedworth

13.3km/8.3miles

A Neolithic long barrow, a Roman villa and a WWII airfield on this fine woodland and field walk with short, steep drops and climbs in and out of Chedworth.

White Way Roman Road » Chedworth Roman Villa » Chedworth Woods » Chedworth » Pinkwell Chambered Cairn » Chedworth » RAF Chedworth » White Way

Start

Roadside parking by gateway on White Way, 3km north–west of Chedworth village. GR: SP 044139.
Take care not to obstruct gateway and remember that large vehicles with trailers may need access. There is other roadside parking south of this gateway.

The Walk

From White Way Roman road, plunge into woodland alongside the disused Midland and South Western Junction Railway then drop to the remains of Chedworth Roman Villa (National Trust), once one of the grandest villas in Britain.

A steady climb on woodland tracks reaches the ridge above Chedworth village; views stretch across the valley to the right, while closer by scabious and knapweeds abound in summer. Now drop to a road and cross the valley at the south-east edge of the village, next crossing pony paddocks and farmland. The route passes just to the right of Pinkwell Chambered Cairn, barely discernable having been ploughed almost flat.

Walking south-west towards Rendcomb airfield, walkers may be treated to a display of aerobatics or wing-walking flights, before the route turns back, following the Macmillan Way to the north-west of Chedworth. Keeping left after the crossroads leads to the church, after which a small path past cottages takes the walker to the Seven Tuns Inn.

Climbing out of the valley the route touches briefly on the outward path before reaching the site of RAF Chedworth; initially used by Spitfires and also home briefly to the headquarters squadron of the Ninth Air Force of the USAAF. Like other ex-airfields it is now used for grazing. The path crosses the runways where scrubby plants push through the concrete and asphalt. The sight of red kite here suggests the habitat makes good hunting for them, although they feed more on carrion. On reaching the road, return to the car between stands of woodland and airfield buildings.

CHEDWORTH

DISTANCE: 13.3KM/8.3MILES » **TOTAL ASCENT:** 260M/853FT » **START GR:** SP 044139 » **TIME:** ALLOW 4.5 HOURS **MAP:** OS EXPLORER OL45, THE COTSWOLDS, 1:25,000 » **REFRESHMENTS:** SEVEN TUNS INN, CHEDWORTH » **NAVIGATION:** STRAIGHTFORWARD.

TRADITIONAL STONE COTTAGES IN CHEDWORTH

09 CHEDWORTH

Directions – Chedworth

S **Walk downhill** on road (car therefore on left). Look for a fingerpost on the left pointing to path over a small stile/rail on the **right**. Follow this narrow path downhill then, as it widens, **right** and uphill. Continue, now roughly level terrain, for 1km until a short drop to a path junction.

2 **Turn left** downhill. After the turn a grubby *Roman Villa* sign may be seen on the left. At villa buildings **keep right** on to and along access road, then **right** into car park entrance (**take care** not to miss as the sign points at your back!), but then continue **straight ahead** on track. Continue for approx. 500m then **ahead** on to path where track turns left. After a few yards, *Monarch's Way* signs on gateposts confirm this is correct. **Ahead** to path junction, and **continue ahead** on Monarch's Way.

3 Cross road and **keep ahead. Ignore** several possible right turns but where track opens out on to a more-used track with a stile on left, **turn right and down**, meeting road. Continue to bottom then uphill. At road junction go **slightly left** and cross into No Through Road (small *Monarch's Way* sticker on post). **Ahead**, keeping on broad track, then **left** then **right** still on broad track passing rear entrances to Bradstone bungalows.

4 At road, continue across into field. Path should cut corner **half right**, to HG in fence. Being horse country, fences move about with great frequency but stay on this line following arrows over stiles and through gates until at rear of house and stables, then cross stile **right** and **continue ahead** across four fields to a road.

5 Cross road, through FG and **half left** across two fields. Leave second field by far corner on to broad clear track across next two fields (duck aeroplanes). At end of second field **turn right** and at field corner **right again**, following track between trees then with field boundary to right (now following Macmillan Way). **Ahead** across fields and small paddock on to farm drive. Cross road at end then cross on to drive and track opposite and **continue ahead** down to village.

6 Cross main road, and take **left fork** to church. Opposite the path to church take the path on **right** down past cottages. If refreshment is required Seven Tuns Inn is ahead, or **turn left** on road and **continue ahead** downhill then up to right bend in road; take HG **half left**.

7 **Climb**, keeping wall to left. **Keep ahead** at junction of paths toward clump of beech trees, after which path meets airfield perimeter track. **Turn left** and, where PF crosses just before bend, **turn right**, aiming for tin roof. Walk across remains of runway; **straight ahead** to road. **Ahead/right** and stay on road for nearly 1km back to the start.

ST ANDREW'S CHURCH, CHEDWORTH

SAPPERTON

10 Sapperton Tunnels

14km/8.7miles

Canal and rail tunnels give focal points and an insight into transport in the eighteenth century as the walk follows rail and water routes through woodland and pasture.

Broad Ride » Sapperton Railway Tunnel » Tarlton » Tunnel House Inn and Coates Portal » Sapperton Canal Tunnel » Sapperton » Daneway Portal » Daneway » Sapperton Wood » Broad Ride

Start

Northern end of Broad Ride, 1km west of Sapperton village. GR: SO 938030.

The Walk

Blue signs both welcome and restrict visitors to the Bathurst Estate, and permit parking of cars and horseboxes by the start of this walk. A path through woods passes the northern portal of the Sapperton railway tunnel, though it can barely be made out through the bushes. This is a working railway, part of the Golden Valley Line between Swindon and Cheltenham. The line of the tunnel is followed south-east past spoil heaps and air shafts to the southern portal.

After a walk along a track the Macmillan Way leads to the hamlet of Tarlton with the St Osmund Chapel of Ease, a charming building with stained glass by Thomas Denny. The door latch is temperamental but it shouldn't be locked. Crossing fields, pass the Tunnel House Inn, the first of three pubs on the walk, close to the Coates portal of the Sapperton (or Thames and Severn) canal tunnel. At 3,817 yards it was the longest tunnel of any kind in England from 1789 to 1811, but, having no towpath, boats could only be propelled by 'legging'. Roof falls have made it unsafe although there were organised boat trips along 300 metres of its length at the Coates end until protected species of bats were found to be roosting there.

Continuing through more of the Bathurst Estate woodlands and now underneath the Golden Valley Line, a road section leads to the village of Sapperton. Passing the The Bell pub and the church a path leads downhill to the Daneway portal at the northern end of the Sapperton canal tunnel. Dank and overgrown, there is little trace of the lengthsman's cottage which still existed into the 1980s. Continue with the course of the canal on the right and the River Frome on the left, and join the road close to the Daneway Inn, before climbing through woodland back to the start.

SAPPERTON TUNNELS

DISTANCE: 14KM/8.7MILES » **TOTAL ASCENT:** 215M/705FT » **START GR:** SO 938030 » **TIME:** ALLOW 4.5 HOURS **MAP:** OS EXPLORER 168, STROUD, TETBURY & MALMESBURY, 1:25,000 » **REFRESHMENTS:** TUNNEL INN, COATES; THE BELL OR THE DANEWAY INN, SAPPERTON » **NAVIGATION:** SOME CARE NEEDED IN WOODS AT BEGINNING AND END OF WALK.

FROSTY FOOTPATH OUTSIDE SAPPERTON

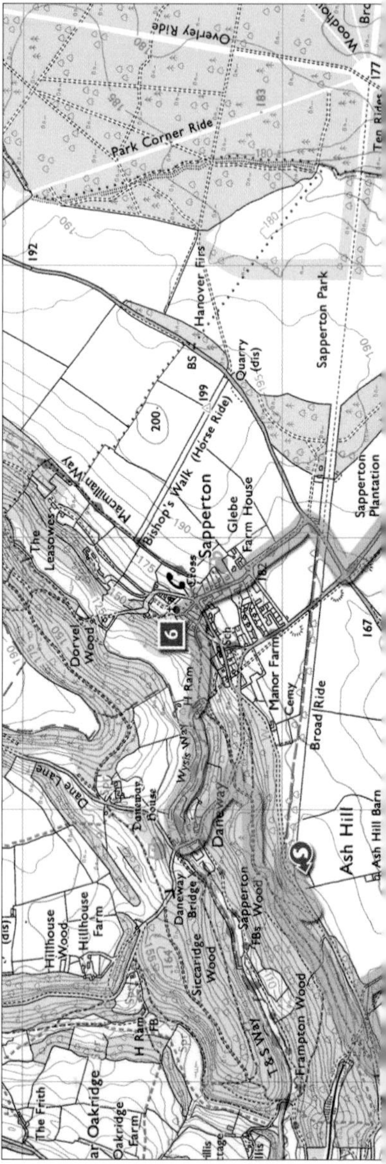

10 SAPPERTON TUNNELS

Directions – Sapperton Tunnels

S➜ From the parking area take the road **slightly downhill** with parking on left. After the muddy passing place on the left **turn right** into woods on an unmarked path. There are many paths in the woods but the aim is to drop to a clear and obvious relatively flat path. The path from the road should go back right and downhill to then meet this flatter path: **turn left**. **Continue ahead** on this main path, muddy at times. After climbing, look for the brick air shaft on the RHS. **Continue** to path junction. **Either continue bearing left** on narrow path to road, **or turn right** and walk downhill for overgrown views of the northern rail tunnel portal of the Golden Valley Line, then retrace your steps and continue to road.

2 **Turn left, then right** on to track at blue *Private Woodlands* sign (**NOT** at the PF sign that comes first). On passing air shafts and aerial mast **keep right** at fork, then follow field/wood boundary to road. Cross into field opposite and **continue ahead** across fields, crossing stile into woodland then **keep right** to reach A419 adjacent to end of railway tunnel.

3 **Turn right** on road then **cross (with care) almost immediately on to track. Continue ahead** for approx. 2km. Where second track crosses at right angles (look for clump of trees across field right and Macmillan Way markers) **turn left**. Leave woodland and walk **half right** aiming for gap in trees with gate, then **continue** on same line through gateway and further gate into green lane. **Straight ahead** to end and hamlet of Tarlton; **turn left** with hedge ahead.

OR **OR**: To visit the St Osmund Chapel of Ease, **turn right** with hedge ahead then **right again** along walled path where signed, before returning to Macmillan Way.

4 Following Macmillan Way **turn right** through gate and **half left** across field to HG then **half right** to stone stile. Look and aim for Tunnel House Inn across fields, passing site of Roman villa, not noticeable from the ground. With inn to left, sign directs down steps to see Coates portal of canal tunnel. Return to car park level and take driveway over tunnel, then **turn left** along track, shortly through gate. **Fork right** under railway bridge and **keep left** at next fork. **Continue ahead** when other paths cross. At field go **straight ahead** to **cross A419 with care** and **ahead** again to unclassified road. **Turn left**.

5 Continue on road to crossroads; **turn right**. **Turn left** at next junction. (Both junctions signed *Sapperton*.) Walk into village passing The Bell pub. At LH bend in road go **ahead** on to hedged path with churchyard on right. At end **turn left** (unless visiting St Kenelm's Church a few metres to the right).

6 Back on route, walk **downhill slightly** past cottages then **steeply down** path **right**. Through KG into field and continue **left** and **downhill** on path. **Cross stile** into woods then over top of canal tunnel and **right**, passing Daneway portal. Follow main raised path with canal on right and River Frome on left, past The Daneway Inn, to road. **Turn left** uphill. After 350m **turn right** on to PF and follow main track. After short downhill then uphill **bear left** at fork to return to road. **Turn left** to return to the start.

COATES PORTAL, SAPPERTON CANAL TUNNEL

SWIFT'S HILL

11 Slad & the Painswick Brook 14km/8.7miles

Woods, fields and streams with a few climbs, giving views of Cotswold villages on steep hillsides, as well as signs of the eighteenth-century woollen industry in old mill buildings, sluices and mill races.

Bulls Cross » Cockshoot » Painswick Brook » Juniper Hill » Slad » Elcombe » Catswood » Down Hill » Longridge Wood » Bulls Cross

Start

Bulls Cross, at side of B4070 1km north of Slad village.
GR: SO 878088.

The Walk

Lovers of Laurie Lee's *Cider with Rosie* will delight in the familiar place names: for anyone else, this is a varied walk with enough hills to quicken the pulse.

From Bulls Cross, the walk follows the Wysis Way through woods and across fields to drop to the Painswick Brook. After a short detour to the edge of Painswick village, the path returns to the brook, passing conversions and remains of some of the twelve cloth mills powered by just this one stream between 1750 and 1820.

Climbing from the valley bottom the track passes over Juniper Hill, part of an SSSI with its disused limestone quarries, ancient beech woodland and calcicole flora, before dropping into Slad, best known through Laurie Lee's evocative account of a Gloucestershire childhood in the 1920s. Rosebank, now one dwelling but then three, is passed, down the bank on the left of the roadway. Lee's grave in the churchyard is only metres from the Woolpack pub.

Crossing to the far side of the Slad valley the walk follows the Laurie Lee Wildlife Way, with some of his poems reproduced on marker posts. Going through fields and passing a pond it climbs to more woodland, then after another poem a sharp down and up through conserved grassland habitat to the Gloucestershire Wildlife Trust-managed Snows Farm. Still climbing and crossing racehorse gallops on Down Hill, the route passes back into woods, plunging to an unexpected lake on the Slad Brook, before climbing steadily to return to Bulls Cross.

SLAD & THE PAINSWICK BROOK

DISTANCE: 14KM/8.7MILES » **TOTAL ASCENT:** 430M/1,411FT » **START GR:** SO 878088 » **TIME:** ALLOW 4.5 HOURS **MAP:** OS EXPLORER 179, GLOUCESTER, CHELTENHAM & STROUD, 1:25,000 » **REFRESHMENTS:** THE WOOLPACK, SLAD » **NAVIGATION:** STRAIGHTFORWARD.

THE VIEW SOUTH TOWARDS STROUD

11 SLAD & THE PAINSWICK BROOK

Directions – Slad & the Painswick Brook

S With parking on your right, walk a few yards north-east along the road. **Turn left** at a fingerpost on to the Wysis Way. **Turn right** at the first lane passing houses of a wide variety of designs. After about 350m **continue ahead** through gate on to track at bottom edge of wood, then leave the wood and the bridlepath at the junction of path, track and road, following road **right** to staggered crossroads and take the stile ahead into pasture land. Walk **half right and downhill** then up to a stile. Continue over next stile then **half left** and through lower FG (with arrow sign). Cross field aiming for bottom corner. Cross streams and bear round to **left** to follow the Painswick Brook.

2 Continue along lower edge of field, and go through gate **bearing left** on track. Where track turns right, walk **ahead** over stile then climb slightly as you cross field. Pass through scrubby area and into another field; walk **half right** and aim for stile in top fence. **Turn left** on to lane and **bear left** at road. **Sharp left** at junction, signed *Sheepscombe* (sign is behind you and may be overgrown). Walk steeply downhill, past Lovedays Mill, and over stream. Where road bends left **go ahead** over stile.

3 **Turn right** and follow stream across fields, along bank of stream, tracks, driveways and across one road for about 1km. When stream turns right but path doesn't, continue on track **ahead** (**NOT** the uphill one), then **take care** not to miss gate **right** into field. Climb the bank and cross field aiming towards farm, but keep buildings on your right. At the field corner cross the stile; **walk left** to end of farm track and **turn right** at road, then cross stone stile **left** on to streamside path, between cypress then beech hedges.

4 Cross fields, staying alongside stream until mill; cross mill stream and **turn left**. Follow driveway up to road; **bear right**. At Sheephouse go **left** over stile and follow path between wall and post-and-rail fence. Cross another stile, then take path **ahead and uphill**. **Turn left** at road then round to **right** signed *Bulls Cross* and *Birdlip*; **almost immediately turn right** through or around gate or CG and climb track, keeping **right** at fork.

5 At top of Juniper Hill **continue downhill** to arrive at road opposite Slad war memorial. **Continue straight across** following round to right. Keep **straight ahead** at junction and continue to junction with main road and *Steanbridge Lane* sign. (After a few metres note path left dropping down to large cottage and sign *Rosebank*. This was Laurie Lee's childhood home.) Continue down road; on right is the church of Holy Trinity, Slad and the site of Lee's grave (easy to find: go through first gate and up to church; grave is on left). Almost opposite the far gate is the Woolpack Inn: dog friendly, local beer.

6 Continue down the road. After the sharp left bend pass barns and after another 300m look out for footpath **left** dropping over stone stile to cut the corner. Back on road continue down The Vatch then uphill. Note the fenceposts on left.

7 Where road bends right go **ahead** on to track then over stile **right**, following path across two fields and into field with pond. **Turn right** alongside pond and stream and over stile. Path bends left then meets driveway of Furners Farm. **Turn right**, uphill, and **left** at road. Continue along road then opposite cottage **drop left** on to first parallel track through trees. At track junction **keep left**, then **right** and next time **left**, maintaining height. Follow track around lower edge of wood with fields to left. Where path forks look for stile and *Laurie Lee Wildlife Way* sign in **left** fence. Cross stile. Across the valley is Snows Farm – this is where you are going.

8 **Half right** and diagonally down two fields and over stile. Look to cross plank bridge, then round to **left** and over stone bridge before climbing up to farm. **Turn left** on to track and continue uphill to road/track junction. Now follow *Restricted Byway* sign **right** and continue up Down Hill. When at top, **straight ahead** across horse gallops to enter woodland by gate. After approx. 200m look for path steeply downhill **left**. (Marked *FOOTPATH* vertically in white (fading) paint on the trunk of a tree to help.) Cross valley bottom and follow broad track for about 800m until it emerges on road. **Bear left** to return to the start.

ST MICHAEL'S CHURCH, DUNTISBOURNE ROUS

12 Winstone & the Duntisbournes 14.5km/9miles

A walk through woods and fields along the River Frome before crossing the watershed to the Dunt Stream as it passes through the pretty Duntisbourne villages.

Winstone » Miserden Park » Edgeworth Mill Farm » Duntisbourne Rous » Middle Duntisbourne » Duntisbourne Leer » Duntisbourne Abbots » Winstone

Start

Parking at St Bartholomew Church, Winstone, 10.5km north-west of Cirencester. Suggest walkers avoid Sunday mornings or check first as there are services at least fortnightly and parking is limited. GR: SO 965094.

The Walk

From St Bartholomew Church at Winstone, roads and fields lead to the lodge and one of the driveways to Miserden Park. With gardens and a nursery open to the public, and a seventeenth-century manor house, Miserden may be worth a visit in its own right, but the walk just skirts its woodland. After a pretty streamside walk alongside the River Frome, cross the watershed to the Duntisbourne villages. Duntisbourne means 'the stream of a man called Dunt', and Dunt appears to have been a Saxon chief.

Duntisbourne Rous, shown on maps as Rouse (a knight called Le Rous owned some of the land following the Norman Conquest), is followed by Middle Duntisbourne and then Duntisbourne Leer, once owned by the abbey of Notre-Dame de Lyre in Normandy. The largest Duntisbourne, Duntisbourne Abbots (one 't' or two? Records vary), is apparently named to differentiate it from the others and is reached along a raised pathway next to the stream.

Passing the spring which was once the village water supply (why do people feel the need to treat it as a wishing well?) and from which flows the Dunt Stream, the final stretch of the walk is through fields along the valley bottom.

The Duntisbournes and Winstone are small, pretty villages: most are proud to have their own church in which there are information sheets. The lychgate at Duntisbourne Abbots is a little engineering gem.

WINSTONE & THE DUNTISBOURNES

DISTANCE: 14.5KM/9MILES » **TOTAL ASCENT:** 220M/722FT » **START GR:** SO 965094 » **TIME:** ALLOW 5 HOURS **MAP:** OS EXPLORER OL45, THE COTSWOLDS, 1:25,000 » **REFRESHMENTS:** NONE ON ROUTE. THE BELL AT SAPPERTON; GOLDEN HEART INN OR ROYAL GEORGE HOTEL, BIRDLIP » **NAVIGATION:** STRAIGHTFORWARD.

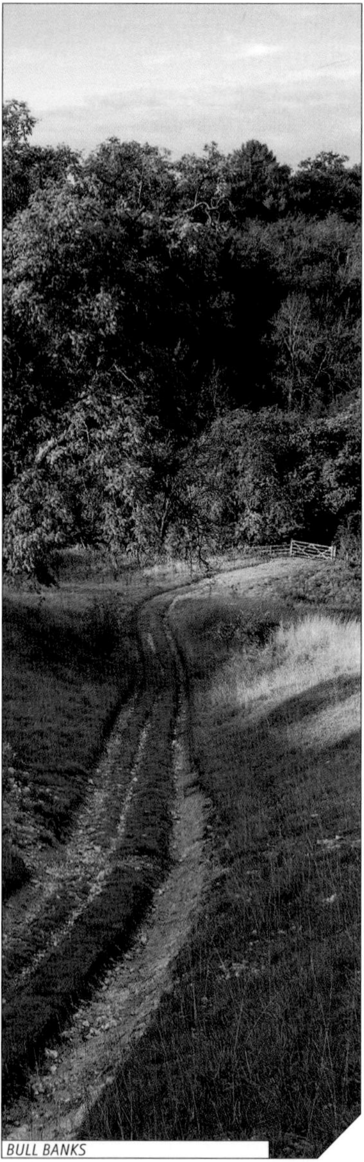

BULL BANKS

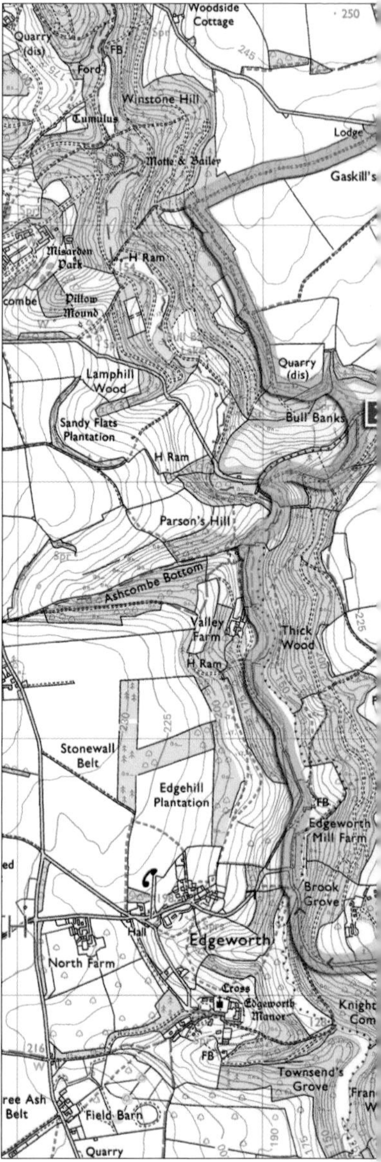

Woodside Cottage
Quarry (dis)
FB
Ford
Winstone Hill
Cumulus
Motte & Bailey
Lodge
Gaskill's
Misarden Park
H Ram
Pillow Mound
Lamphill Wood
Quarry (dis)
Bull Banks
Sandy Flats Plantation
H Ram
Parson's Hill
Ashcombe Bottom
Valley Farm
Thick Wood
H Ram
Stonewall Belt
Edgehill Plantation
FB
Edgeworth Mill Farm
Brook Grove
Hall
Edgeworth
North Farm
Cross
Edgeworth Manor
FB
Townsend's Grove
Belt
Field Barn
Quarry

12 WINSTONE & THE DUNTISBOURNES

Directions – Winstone & the Duntisbournes

S Leave Winstone church via the road. At end of Croft Road, **turn left** on to PF, walking **half right** across field to gates in corner. **Cross stile** and walk **half right** across second field towards farm. At road, **straight ahead** along side road opposite. **Turn left** at lodge on to private drive and **straight ahead** until drive bends right; here take path **left** into woods. Stay in or at left edge of woods for approx. 1km, still following boundary where field/wood boundary turns left passing very small disused quarry. At next corner follow arrows **right** steeply down steps, over stile and out into field, then follow field gully **right** to road.

2 Cross on to track opposite. Walk uphill ahead, **bearing right** at both grass triangles, then downhill, through gate out of woods. Before reaching road at bottom **turn left** on a path/track to a gate leading into woodland. Follow streamside path keeping **right** (downhill) at fork and through/over (probably) wet bit to bridge. **Straight ahead** along this field regardless of plethora of arrows on gate to right. Continue alongside stream over three fields, rising **half right** in third field to a FG with a blue arrow leading on to tarmac driveway. **Bear left** and follow to end. **Turn left** on road. Stay on this road steeply up passing Duntisbourne House on the left to a crossroads.

3 **Turn right** then after 280m **turn left** on to PB. At end of field **turn right** along line of beech trees, then at end **turn left** on to Macmillan Way to gate. Cross road staying with clearly defined and mostly fenced Macmillan Way to road.

4 **Turn right**. A rustic sign on the right will indicate *Saxon Church*, but ignore this for now and remain on road. **Turn left** by The Rectory signed *No Through Road*. This is Duntisbourne Rous. Road leads to a ford; **before this** and before the cottages, **turn left** on PF through a wooden gate to the church. Leave the churchyard by a stile over the stone wall in the opposite corner to that by which you entered, along a narrow path through trees, then down across a field. In next field aim across the middle but look out for a green metal gate on its own (depending on crop situation!) with a stile a few metres behind. After stile, **turn left** on track then **right** down road. You are now in Middle Duntisbourne, but only briefly because where road bends back to right there are three tracks/driveways on **left**. Take the **middle** of these, soon bearing **right** on to path which emerges on to road.

5 **Turn right** and stay on this road for about 1km. **Turn right** signed *Duntisbourne Leer*, then **left** signed *Unsuitable for Motor Vehicles* alongside stream on raised path and into Duntisbourne Abbots.

6 Go ahead on roads to pass telephone kiosk and then church on left. **Fork right** at triangle signed *Birdlip* and *Cirencester*. Walk downhill then **left** over stile into field. Follow valley bottom along two fields then through HG. Cross concrete track through another HG. Back in fields, continue to follow LH boundary then valley bottom round to right between trees. After trees, **bear slight right** to gates and **right** on road to the start.

CRICKLEY HILL, BY BARROW WAKE

13 Brimpsfield & Birdlip

15.8km/9.8miles

From a viewpoint on the Cotswold escarpment, a wide sweep of fields and tracks passes through a river valley to the village of Brimpsfield then returns through beech woods along the Cotswold Way.

Barrow Wake » Stockwell » Brimpsfield Park » Brimpsfield » Birdlip Hill and The Peak » Barrow Wake

Start

Parking at Barrow Wake viewpoint, accessed from the B4070 north of Birdlip. Suggest the car park is used as the on-road parking on the approach road is used by visitors with a 'different' interest.

GR: SO 931153.

The Walk

Barrow Wake derives its name from the find, in 1879, of three skeletons in a stone-lined grave, thought to date from the Iron Age. The land is, like Crickley Hill to the north, designated as a Site of Special Scientific Interest (SSSI), especially notable for its population of musk orchids.

From Barrow Wake an easy, flat stroll along a broad, open track takes you to the edge of the small hamlet of Stockwell, before field, wood and track leads back to and under the A417.

Now through field and wood on the Brimpsfield Park estate before following the River Frome and then climbing to the village with its twelfth-century church, and the earthworks – all that remain of the castle, demolished on the orders of Edward II. From the village another flat and straight walk drops into beech woods – perfect in early May with bluebells, wood anemone and the light, bright green of the new beech leaves.

After a road crossing, the path joins the Cotswold Way with a short diversion to The Peak with views across to the Malvern Hills, before returning along the escarpment to the car park.

BRIMPSFIELD & BIRDLIP

DISTANCE: 15.8KM/9.8MILES » **TOTAL ASCENT:** 280M/919FT » **START GR:** SO 931153 » **TIME:** ALLOW 5 HOURS
MAP: OS EXPLORER 179, GLOUCESTER CHELTENHAM & STROUD, 1:25,000 » **REFRESHMENTS:** GOLDEN HEART, NETTLETON; ROYAL GEORGE, BRIMPSFIELD; THE AIR BALLOON AT A417/A436 JCT » **NAVIGATION:** STRAIGHTFORWARD.

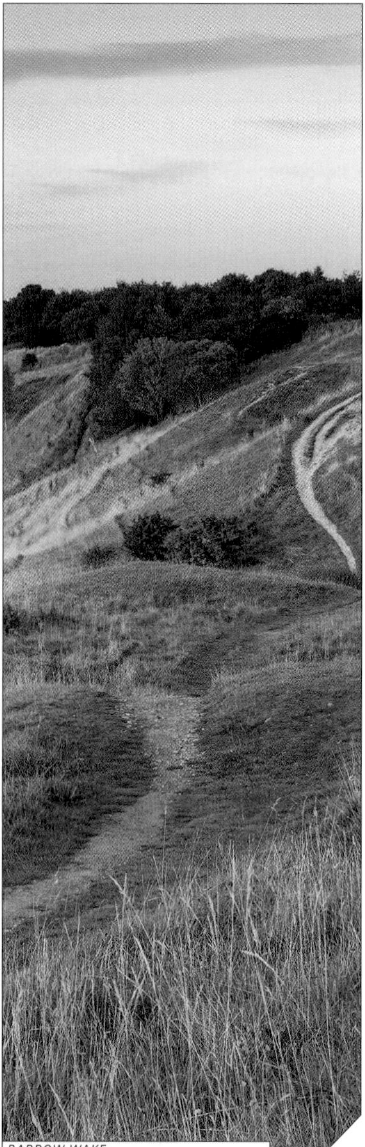

BARROW WAKE

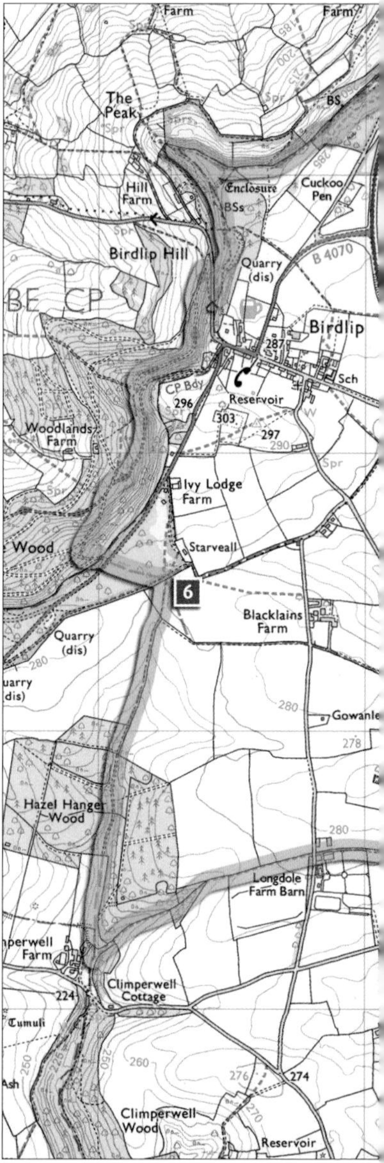
Farm
Farm
The Peak
Spr
Hill Farm
Enclosure
BSs
Cuckoo Pen
BS
Birdlip Hill
Quarry (dis)
B 4070
BE CP
Birdlip
287
Sch
CP Bdy
296
Reservoir
303
297
290
Woodlands Farm
Ivy Lodge Farm
Wood
Starveall
6
Blacklains Farm
Quarry (dis)
280
uarry (dis)
Gowanle
278
Hazel Hanger Wood
Longdole Farm Barn
perwell Farm
Climperwell Cottage
224
Tumuli
250
225
260
276
274
270
Ash
Climperwell Wood
Reservoir

13 BRIMPSFIELD & BIRDLIP

Directions – Brimpsfield & Birdlip

S Leaving the car park by the road, **turn left** under the A417 then take the PF **right** at the wide gated track and continue for almost 1.5km to a road. **Turn right** to the edge of the hamlet of Stockwell, then **left** on to the concrete drive immediately before the farm. **Straight ahead** on this track for about 1km until faced with a gate. **Go right** through HG and follow round to left, then **ahead** to road. **Turn left.**

2 **Turn right**, marked as PF. Follow drive to cottage garden wall, then **right** and **left** around garden and wood boundary. Where there is a nick in the woodland with a view left to Cowley Manor Hotel, continue a few metres into next field then cross **half right** to road. **Ahead** into side road and, where road bends left, **straight ahead** signed *PB*, alongside wall. At field corner, leave wall and cross field following same line. Aim for FG adjacent to main road once it becomes visible. Through gate and **turn right. Turn left** under the A417 road, **left** through HG then **right** on to path between wall and fence.

3 Stay close to left boundary through second field and at end pick up track going **half right** and downhill. Stay on track then at lake and weir **turn right** to cross second FB and up into field. Follow arrow round to left and, on reaching track, follow downhill back to recross stream; **almost immediately** leave track and **turn right** into trees alongside stream. Path becomes indistinct but continue alongside stream, over a broken wall until treehouse. **Walk left** up steps on to drive then a seemingly pointless diversion **right** almost through a cottage bedroom! Back on to driveway and **ahead** to road. **Turn left.**

4 Uphill, round bend, then **immediately after** track/driveway on left, cross over stile into field on **left**, aiming for left telegraph pole. After stile, PF goes to right but worn path makes a shortcut to church. Note earthwork remains of castle on far side of track.

5 From church, track back to lane then **left** and **left** again at war memorial and **right** into The Knapp. Take PF on **right** between walls, **straight ahead** across field and ahead on to track. **Keep ahead** and cross lane at Longdole Polo Club, still **ahead**. Enter corner of woodland and follow path down to gate. **Keep ahead** across field by RH boundary and over two stiles, then **sharp right** through FG to go back along boundary of the wood you've just left. Keeping roughly to the hollow, walk back into more beech woods, along right edge of one field, through HG ahead and **half left** across field to gate in wall.

6 **Turn left** and after about 30m **half right** to angle away from wood boundary. At road look **right** and a few metres along is a PF sign on the other side. Take the most downhill option, round to **right** and continue down to meet the Cotswold Way. **Bear right**. Follow Cotswold Way through the woods (watching out for **left** turn off main track) then still on Cotswold Way **sharp right** up steps to cross a road. Continuing more gently up to fingerpost. Weather depending it's worth the short out-and-back diversion to see the view from The Peak. Return to Cotswold Way and, after path leaves woods the parking area at the start can be seen a little distance ahead and up.

LOOKING OUT OVER THE M5

MEANDERING FOOTPATH THROUGH CHARLTON ABBOTS

14 Belas Knap & the Beesmoor Brook

17.5km/10.9miles

Winchcombe Church and Sudeley Castle to the Neolithic Belas Knap long barrow, joined by a valley walk and the villages of Charlton Abbots and Brockhampton.

Corndean Lane » Winchcombe outskirts » Sudeley Castle » Beesmoor Brook » Charlton Abbots » Brockhampton » Sevenhampton Church » Belas Knap » Corndean Lane

Start

Roadside parking on Corndean Lane, 2km south of Winchcombe.
GR: SP 021262.

The Walk

Crossing the fields behind Winchcombe gives good views of St Peter's, one of the great wool churches of the Cotswolds, before the walk enters the grounds of Sudeley Castle, final resting place of Katherine Parr after her short marriage to Thomas Seymour, 1st Baron Seymour of Sudeley, having survived Henry VIII. From the front of the castle the path drops to the Beesmoor Brook then crosses several fields. A climb into Charlton Abbots, site of a former leper colony, is followed by another walk across fields to Brockhampton where The Craven Arms pub provides boxes in the hallway for muddy boots, but welcomes dogs. The nineteenth-century mansion at Brockhampton Park is now split into flats.

Farmland leads to Sevenhampton, then a steady climb to higher country is accompanied by skylarks and quite possibly a strong breeze. After a short diversion across farmland and an old quarry as an alternative to road walking, a broad track meets up with the Cotswold Way, continuing to Belas Knap long barrow, a Neolithic burial chamber where the remains of at least thirty-eight people were found during excavations in the 1860s and again between 1928 and 1930. This barrow has been restored, giving a good indication of its original profile; the information board on site explains it further. From Belas Knap it is a downhill walk across two fields to return to the start.

BELAS KNAP & THE BEESMOOR BROOK

DISTANCE: 17.5KM/10.9MILES » **TOTAL ASCENT:** 315M/1,033FT » **START GR:** SP 021262 » **TIME:** ALLOW 5 HOURS
MAP: OS EXPLORER OL45, THE COTSWOLDS, 1:25,000; OS LANDRANGER 163, CHELTENHAM & CIRENCESTER, 1:50,000
REFRESHMENTS: CRAVEN ARMS, BROCKHAMPTON » **NAVIGATION:** STRAIGHTFORWARD.

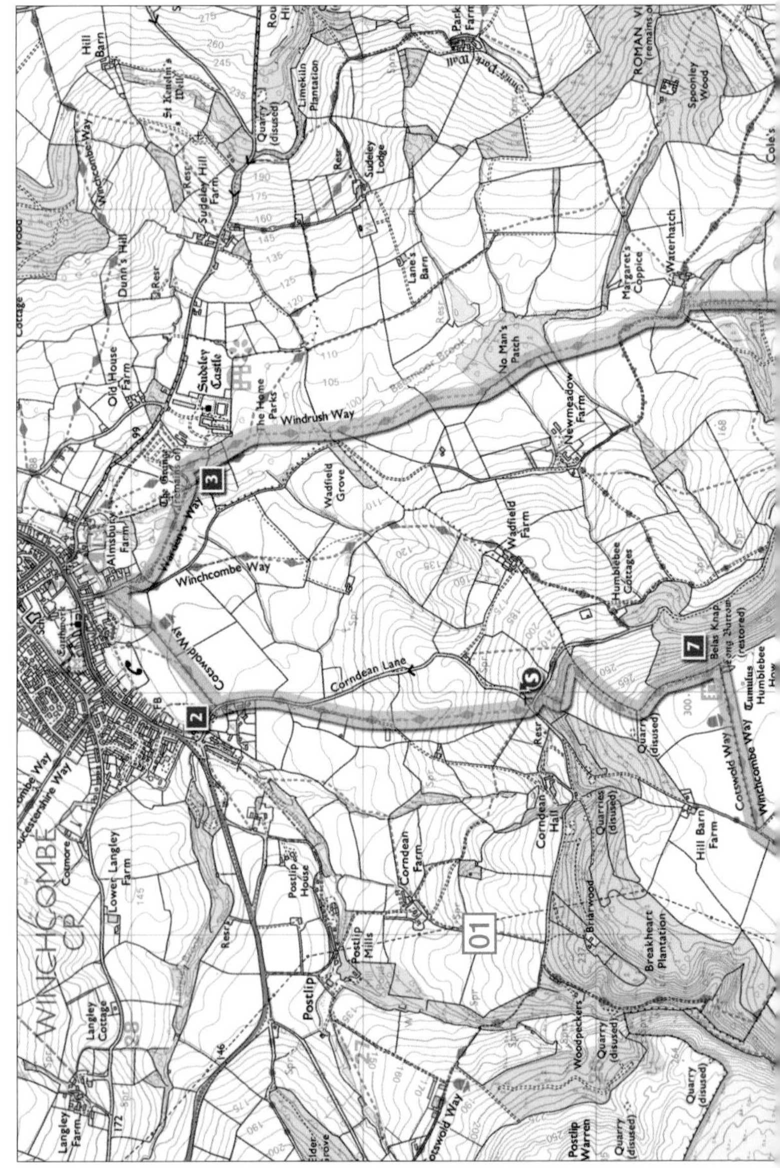

WINCHCOMBE CP
Winchcombe Way
Gloucestershire Way
Cotswold Way
Windrush Way
Warden's Way
Corndean Lane
Sudeley Castle
The Home Parks
Almsbury Farm
Old House Farm
Dunn's Hill
Sudeley Hill Farm
St Kenelm's Well
Hill Barn
Quarry (disused)
Limekiln Plantation
Sudeley Lodge
Lane's Barn
Park Farm
Margaret's Coppice
Waterhatch
ROMAN VI
Spoonley Wood
No Man's Patch
Beesmoor Brook
Newmeadow Farm
Wadfield Grove
Wadfield Farm
Humblebee Cottages
Belas Knap Long Barrow (restored)
Tumulus
Humblebee How
Hill Barn Farm
Corndean Hall
Quarries (disused)
Corndean Farm
Briarwood
Breakheart Plantation
Postlip House
Postlip Mills
Postlip
Woodpeckers
Postlip Warren
Lower Langley Farm
Langley Cottage
Langley Farm
Cotmore
Earthwork
Sch
FB
Resr
2
3
5
7
01

14 BELAS KNAP & THE BEESMOOR BROOK

Directions – Belas Knap & the Beesmoor Brook

S Walk downhill to the road junction, taking Cotswold Way **ahead** through gate and down (rough) centre of field. **Right** on to track and continue towards Winchcombe. **Bear left** on to public road. Stay on Cotswold Way, **turning right** on to track.

2 Continue along left field and stream boundaries following Cotswold Way to road (Vineyard Street). **Turn right** then **continue ahead** through entrance to Sudeley Castle; follow drive towards the car park. After adventure playground on the right, go through HG keeping playground on right. If you reach the car park you've missed it.

3 **Ahead** into field, staying close to top boundary until fence, then strike off **half right** and downhill to exit field at far bottom corner. **Right** over stream then **left** signed *Windrush Way*. Cross two fields, aiming for the top corner of a wood, and continue over several stiles with the wood to your left. Cross small stream into field, and **straight across** to fingerpost. **Turn left** down track, through gate. **Stay left** on track to cross stream then **turn right**. Follow track keeping stream and woodland on your right, then leave track **right** through gate to stay adjacent to stream/woodland. Unfortunately there are no PF markers. Watch for row of conifers and Holt Farm on left skyline. Level with this farm, **turn right** over stile and take path across a small dam. Exiting woodland go **half left** aiming for LHS of Charlton Abbots church.

4 Pass to **left** of church and continue to lane. **Turn left** to road, **stay left/ahead** and follow lane to T-junction. **Turn left**, signed *Guiting Power* and *Naunton* and after a few metres, at end of coppice, **turn right** on to footpath which goes **left** close to field boundary. At far top-left corner, arrow on post directs walkers through gap and forwards with boundary at first on RHS across fields to Brockhampton. On reaching road, **continue ahead** past village hall, bearing **right** then **left** to the Craven Arms.

5 Continue on from the Craven Arms. Follow fingerpost for Sevenhampton down and across stream (the infant River Coln). Enter field, go **left** and uphill towards farm. Keep buildings on your RHS through KGs behind Manor Farm and the Manor House into the new churchyard and through to the old. After leaving the church **turn right**. At road T-junction, **straight ahead** on to track then fields. **Turn right** at the road.

6 With road junction in sight ahead, follow PF sign **left** with boundary to your RHS through several fields going downhill, over stiles then back up through a marshy area. Now **half left** and with boundary now on your left continue to a gate and stile on the left where several paths appear to meet. **Do not cross stile** but, turning your back on the gate, walk to **left** of scrubby trees, which leads to the top edge of another wood. On and through fields keeping to edge of woodland until double gate/corral. Here you enter final field, a disused and overgrown quarry. Cross field **half right** to rejoin road. **Turn left**. Where road ends at parking area **continue** on to track. **Straight ahead**. After passing between barns, **bear half right**, remaining on track. Cotswold Way joins from left but go **ahead**, continuing on Cotswold Way for remainder of walk. **Take care** not to miss **right turn** off track into field to Belas Knap.

7 After exploring this Neolithic long barrow, and with your back to the stone stile where you entered the Belas Knap enclosure, exit enclosure by another stone stile in front of you and **turn ninety degrees left** through iron KG, through small trees with fence to right, and on into next field. Continue with fence to right to bottom of field and walk half of bottom field boundary until gate and signs lead **right** and steeply down through woods to emerge at the start.

INSIDE THE NEOLITHIC LONG BARROW AT BELAS KNAP

SECTION 3

The South Cotswolds

The limestone outcrop narrows towards the south of the Cotswolds and the villages are more influenced by the city of Bath and the M4 corridor. In general, the walking involves more hills; certainly more than in the north-east Cotswolds. There is more evidence of traditional agriculture – more cattle and sheep, and barley and root crops. There are also many horses: horses for eventing, racing and hunting. These use the bridleways, but as well as making them muddy, they certainly help to keep the paths open.

THE TYNDALE MONUMENT ON NIBLEY KNOLL (ROUTE 16)

THE VIEW WEST FROM COALEY PEAK (ROUTE 19)

NEWINGTON FARM, NEWINGTON BAGPATH

15 Lasborough & Ozleworth Bottom 12.2km/7.6miles

Deep, damp wooded valleys and country houses which seem to have sprung from the soil itself. Horses for the hunting and pheasants for the shooting. Approve or not, it's the hunting, shooting landowners who keep these estates in good repair.

Ozleworth » Ozleworth Bottom » Lasborough » Newington Bagpath » Marlees Brook » Ozleworth

Start

Parking off road close to bend in Ozleworth, 4km east of Wotton-under-Edge. GR: ST 792935.

The Walk

This walk goes through privately owned Ozleworth Park (gardens open on occasions under the National Gardens Scheme) to Ozleworth Bottom following the stream through damp woodland – at certain times it feels like walking underwater through kelp beds.

Emerging on to pasture, a climb crosses the drive of Lasborough Park, designed by James Wyatt in the 1790s. Here there are views across the valley to Lasborough Farm and church. Soon cross the valley and explore tiny Lasborough Church which featured in the TV series *Lark Rise to Candleford*; look back for views of Lasborough Park with its embattled parapet and four corner towers. On the plateau the field path passes a horseshoe-shaped motte, then drops back into the valley and the hamlet of Newington Bagpath. Planning permission was granted in 2013 for the church to be converted to a dwelling but progress is slow. After fields drop into the valley of Marlees Brook. Both Ozleworth and Marlees are managed to raise pheasant for shooting, and young birds or poults by the hundred if not thousand may run, fly, squawk and flap from under your feet.

The path climbs to skirt the house at Ozleworth Park but the church of St Nicholas of Myra can be visited. It is one of only two in Gloucestershire to have a hexagonal tower, and its situation in a circular yard suggests the site has very early if not pre-Christian origins.

LASBOROUGH & OZLEWORTH BOTTOM

DISTANCE: 12.2KM/7.6MILES » **TOTAL ASCENT:** 270M/886FT » **START GR:** ST 792935 » **TIME:** ALLOW 3.5 HOURS **MAP:** OS EXPLORER 168, STROUD, TETBURY & MALMESBURY, 1:25,000 » **REFRESHMENTS:** HUNTER'S HALL INN, KINGSCOTE » **NAVIGATION:** STRAIGHTFORWARD.

OZLEWORTH BOTTOM

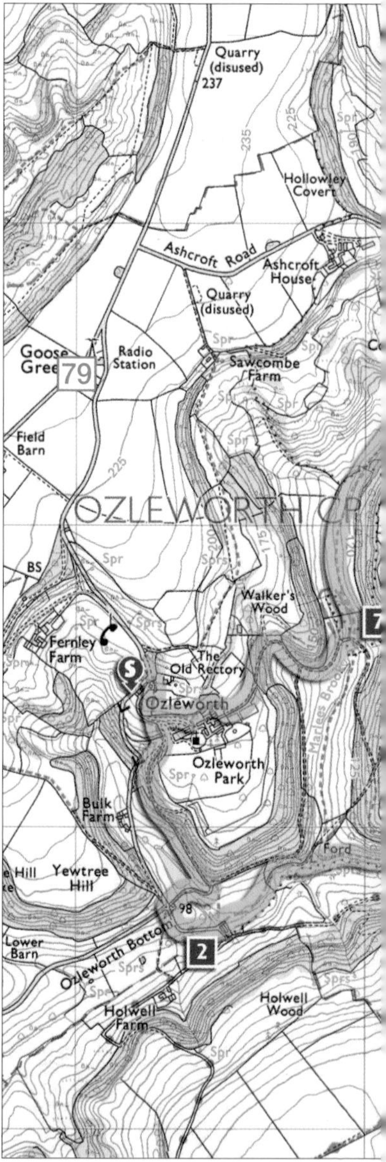

KINGSCOTE CP
Newington Bagpath
Lasborough
Bagpath
Boxwell
15 LASBOROUGH & OZLEWORTH BOTTOM

Directions – Lasborough & Ozleworth Bottom

S On the point of the bend, take the centre path (gate and stone stile) signed *Church* and *Bridle Path*. At tarmac drive go **right** and at end of hedge **left** through gate. **Half left** towards house to cut field corner, on to drive **keeping right** and downhill all the way to the lodge. Exit through electrically controlled gates. **Turn left** and downhill, signed *Unsuitable for motors*.

2 At RH bend, before cottage, **ahead** through gate and **ahead** in field, later aiming **half left** to gate signed *PB*. Drop into trees ahead on often-muddy path, and **keep right** on main track over FB/ford. **Ahead** keeping to track along valley bottom, eventually rising to cross a track, and now passing between stone gateposts. **Keep left** with hollow/clearing/pond on right. Follow path to **left** at end, continuing about 300m to another probably superfluous FB then climbing with the stream now on the left. At next hollow/clearing/pond (depends how wet it has been), **keep right** and pass bamboo, keeping on main track and exiting woodland through a gate.

3 Follow track; after a while it will rise and cross a metalled drive. Now **ahead** climbing to corner of wood and on to field corner before contouring round to right to the end boundary wall with a gate and PF signs. **Do not pass through** but go back **right**, keeping downhill between stands of trees and curving round **left** to meet lane. **Turn left**, over CG and climb into Lasborough. Church is on the right.

4 Continue uphill, round LH bend and **turn left** into field by PF sign. Pass to LHS of motte to gate at top field corner. After gate, **half left** and down, meeting track and continuing **ahead** to follow wall on left through gate into field. Aim across field and downhill to gate with stone shed to its side. Exit field **left** on to track and **ahead** steeply up past disused Newington Bagpath church.

5 After church enter field **left**, walking back towards church and keeping boundary on left to PF sign. **Turn hard right** across field aiming for Ozleworth radio station mast (or towards far corner if it's foggy). **Right** in field corner, keeping boundary wall on left, to end of field. **Turn right** on to road.

6 **Ahead** past post box to junction. **Keep left** then **left** through gate marked *Restricted Byway*. Steep and slippery path down. After gate, **left** around wall to second gate, then **right** downhill between post and rail fences. **Exact route now unclear** and arrow on post is broken, but continue steeply down and curve **left** to valley bottom and gate. Follow path along valley bottom. After trees on right end, look for a substantial stone bridge over the stream.

7 Cross bridge and continue, with stream now on left, to a track. **Keep right**, now climbing. **Ahead** on main path to stone entrance to Ozleworth House, then follow PB **right**. Follow round to **left** past pond. **Left** to visit church, otherwise continue on path and **turn right** at second PB sign to return to the start.

NEWINGTON BAGPATH

16 Wotton-under-Edge & North Nibley

12.6km/7.8miles

Down and up the Cotswold Edge with stunning views over the Severn.

Old London Road » Wotton-under-Edge » Holywell » Coombe » Waterley Bottom » Pitt Court » North Nibley » Tyndale Monument » Old London Road

Start

Roadside parking in Old London Road. GR: ST 754940.

The Walk

At first through woodland, the walk drops into Wotton-under-Edge, a charitable town with four sets of almshouses all of which are passed on the route: first Streamsfield, the original Rowland Hill Almshouses built in 1815 and now private residences, then the 'new' Rowland Hill buildings (1887). Down Wotton's main shopping street into Church Street where Perry & Dawes Almshouses welcome visitors through the arch into the courtyard where a tiny chapel stands. After the church, a short loop passes Ann Bearpackers Almshouses.

Leave Wotton on a dog-walkers' path beside a stream which in the nineteenth-century powered several woollen mills, to the hamlets of Holywell and Coombe then climb up the escarpment by a sheep track and back down through woods and fields. Another short streamside walk and quiet lanes lead to the village of North Nibley with its community-run village shop and the Black Horse Inn.

Climb again through beech woods to the optional extra of the 121 steps of the Tyndale Monument, built to commemorate the Bible translator William Tyndale who was born nearby and martyred at Flanders in 1536. Follow the Cotswold Way through woods for a while before diverting to Wotton Hill with its clump of trees first planted following the Battle of Waterloo in 1815. Back into the woods for a short walk back to the start.

WOTTON-UNDER-EDGE & NORTH NIBLEY

DISTANCE: 12.6KM/7.8MILES » **TOTAL ASCENT:** 320M/1,050FT » **START GR:** ST 754940 » **TIME:** ALLOW 3.5 HOURS
MAP: OS EXPLORER 167, THORNBURY, DURSLEY & YATE, 1:25,000 » **REFRESHMENTS:** BLACK HORSE INN, NORTH NIBLEY; NORTH NIBLEY VILLAGE SHOP » **NAVIGATION:** STRAIGHTFORWARD.

NIBLEY KNOLL

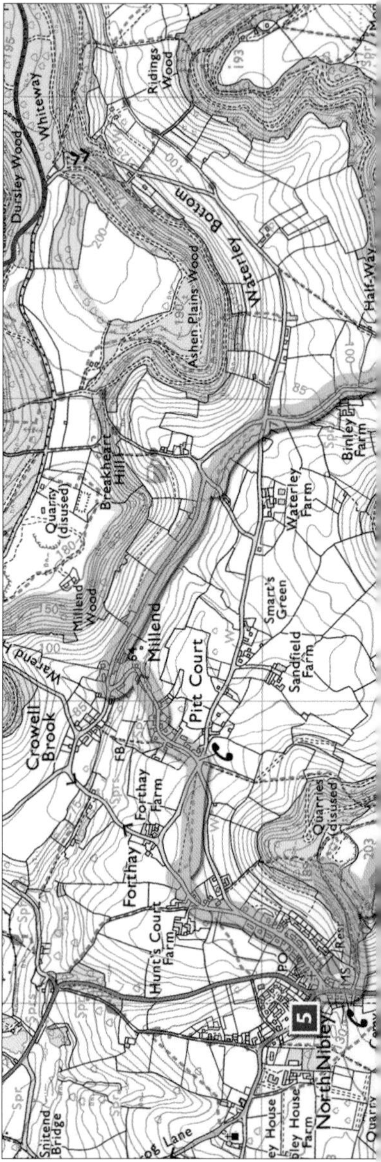

16 WOTTON-UNDER-EDGE & NORTH NIBLEY

Directions – Wotton-under-Edge & North Nibley

S Look for the signed footpath into the woods opposite the car parking. **Bear left** and follow through to road. **Turn left** uphill then at junction **hard right** over stile into woods. **Bear right** on to track then **right downhill** at both first and second forks, down steps and continue to road. **Turn left**. After a few metres, **turn right** and follow PF down field, between trees and round to left along narrow enclosed path passing Streamsfield cottages on right (the original Rowland Hill Almshouses). Continue across estate hammerhead and up past Tabernacle Chapel. **Ahead** downhill passing new Rowland Hill Almshouses on left. **Quick right** and **left** at junction into Bear Street, then **left** into High Street.

2 Follow road **left** into Church Street (with Perry & Dawes Almshouses through arch on right). **Across** at junction past telephone kiosk and church. Just after Parklands junction, opposite church, take path **left** marked *Leading to Bear Packer Alms Houses* which are on the right. **Turn right** at road, back to main road, then **left** then **right** steeply down The Cedars. **Left** then along streamside path. At road **quick right** then **left**, signed *Cotswold Way* and still streamside.

3 At road **turn left**, then **half right** at cottages, now climbing. **Keep left** at next junction through hamlet of Coombe, and **keep right**. Pass sign *Sharp turn Unsuitable for motors* then **left** still uphill to meet main road. **Cross with care** on to PB climbing hillside. Continue to road; **straight across** again on to path marked *PB to Spuncombe Bottom*. At fork and *Laycombe Wood* sign **keep right**, then **fork left** steeply and carefully down a path often scoured by rainwater. **Ahead** on narrow hedge-lined path to road. **Turn right**.

4 After 500m at a junction with an obvious track on right, **turn right** then **immediately left** through gate and follow left field boundary (beware of holes/badger setts!) to gateway back on to road by cottage. **Turn right** to crossroads, then over gate **diagonally opposite** into field, walking to tree then following stream. Cross stile on to road. **Turn right** up to junction and then **left**. Stay on road, then **turn left** at next junction, steeply down and up. At grass triangle go **right** taking gate and PF into field in-between the two roads. Follow well-used dog path to stile at far side. **Turn left** on road and **right** at junction into North Nibley (shop and pub).

5 Past pub, **turn left** then follow Cotswold Way sign **left** uphill on wooded track/path. Follow Cotswold Way signs which may change, having already had temporary re-route due to landslip. Whichever path used will lead to Tyndale Monument.

6 Continue around field perimeter with drop on RHS. Entering woods, follow Cotswold Way signs staying on main track. Take note when the woods on LHS give way to a field (just after large pile of logs, though these may one day move) and at the next Cotswold Way PB sign (blue arrow) **leave Cotswold Way** on to near-parallel path on **right**. Continue, still keeping the drop close on RHS, but keep on the flat, ignoring obvious downhill path. About 400m from blue arrow (above), **turn sharp left** on to a path up a rough bank and then **right** through KG at top. Walk down field to RHS of walled trees, with seats and views.

7 Continue anti-clockwise round enclosure to go back into woods uphill and **right**. Through KG, follow this path as far as possible, avoiding the road on the right. Path returns to start.

BRIDLEWAY ON COOMBE HILL

HINTON HILL, NEAR DYRHAM PARK

17 Dyrham & West Littleton

12.9km/8miles

Easy walking over fields and along the Cotswold Way, views from the escarpment towards Bristol and the Severn, and the National Trust's Dyrham Park and the village of West Littleton.

A46 » Dyrham Park » Sands Farm » A46 » West Littleton » A46 » Beacon Lane Plantation » Cotswold Way » Dyrham Park » A46

Start

Lay-by on western side of A46, 3km south of M4 junction 18. GR: ST 749754. Please do not try to cross the A46 to use the lay-by if travelling from the north as there have been too many nasty accidents along this stretch of the road. The next junction on the right (to Dyrham) is wide and easy for turning, then approach from the south.

The Walk

A public footpath down through the National Trust's Dyrham Park gives glimpses of the house and quite possibly some of the 200 fallow deer in the park, before the walk picks up the Cotswold Way south for a short distance.

It's then a climb through pony paddocks and arable fields to cross the busy A46, after which more fields along the ridge lead to the village of West Littleton, a beautiful hamlet with links to famous film stars and Olympians. The stars move on; the village remains. The churchyard is the final resting place of the Olympian equestrian Richard Meade (1938–2015) whose son continues to train and school horses in the village. This is also a lovely spot for a sandwich.

The walk continues along tracks and fields, recrossing the busy A46 to follow the Cotswold Way back to Dyrham village, passing directly behind the house and garden. St Peter's, the church at Dyrham, may also be visited; it is still in regular use as a place of worship and is not, although it may look like it, part of the National Trust property.

A steady climb back through the parkland retraces the outward route back to the start.

DYRHAM & WEST LITTLETON

DISTANCE: 12.9KM/8MILES » **TOTAL ASCENT:** 245M/804FT » **START GR:** ST 749754 » **TIME:** ALLOW 4 HOURS **MAP:** OS EXPLORER 155, BRISTOL & BATH, 1:25,000 » **REFRESHMENTS:** THE TOLLGATE TEASHOP ON A46 » **NAVIGATION:** STRAIGHTFORWARD.

GATE IN WEST LITTLETON

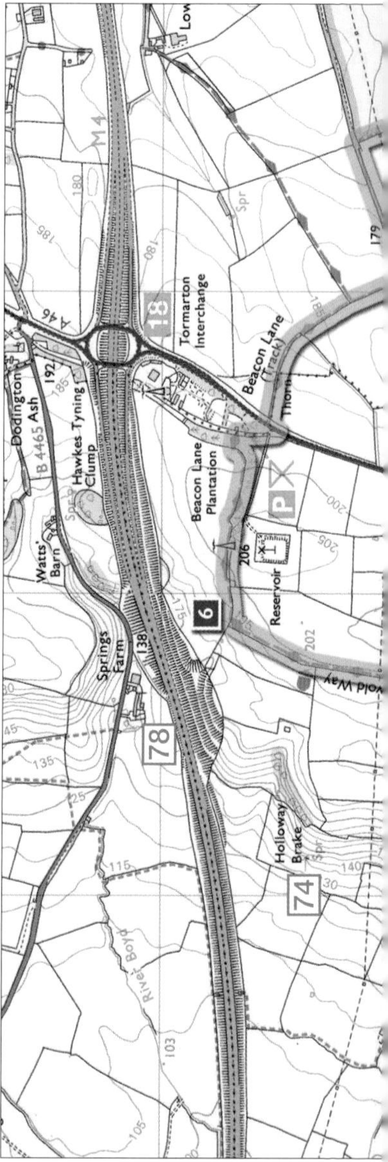

17 DYRHAM & WEST LITTLETON

Directions – Dyrham & West Littleton

S Walk along the verge with the wall to your left and **turn left** over stone steps and through a squeeze stile. **Straight ahead** through a metal gate then across parkland following line of deer fence. Enter woodland, follow path then emerge on to road. **Turn right** downhill, pass driveway to Sands Farm, **turn left** and, immediately before Dyrham village sign, **turn left** on to Cotswold Way.

2 At first option, leave Cotswold Way and cross stile **left**, climbing field. Enter second field by KG and climb to farm drive, crossing **ahead** up steps and keeping to field edge through tree belt at right side. Again **ahead** to field corner crossing track to stile. **Do not cross stile** but turn with your back to stile and follow arrow now **half left** to a break in hedge and trees above (marker post may be visible). On reaching busy A46 road note Tollgate teashop to the right but **turn left**, **crossing with care** and **take first right** (road with signed 7.5T limit).

3 At end of trees, **turn left** over stone stile then gate, now keeping boundary on RHS towards barn. (Yes, that is your car you can see on the left.) Pass barn, keeping to this hedge/fence/wall line through gates and gaps until choice is only left (over horse jump and ladder stile) or right. **Turn right** through gateway and ahead across field, bearing **right** at end to HG which leads to stone stile into West Littleton churchyard.

4 After exploring church, return via same stone stile, and part way through wood look for path **left** to another stile. Keep to left edge of field to horse chestnut tree; **turn left** over another stone stile and follow path between hedge and wall to road. **Turn left**. Walk through West Littleton village. After telephone kiosk take **second** road **right** past cottages, continuing on to track. After dip and stream, go through gate **right**. Map suggests path cuts field corner but the stile at top is impassable. Keep to left edge of field to track and there **turn right**. Take PF on **left** then **half right** across field to gap, then aim for left side of trees at field boundary ahead. As you go over brow another wall becomes visible: a short distance to left of the gap take stone stile, still heading for LHS of trees. Stile has gone from next boundary but climb grassed-over wall into field and now aim for hedge corner ahead, to the right of pylon.

5 At corner, continue towards and eventually beneath pylon to road. **Turn left**. Immediately after electricity lines have crossed road (about 450m) **turn right**, continuing **ahead** where the Cotswold Way joins from right. **Straight ahead** to A46. **Please cross with care** at the island, then take the slip road opposite. Enter the woods **left** at the Cotswold Way sign. Go straight through woods then follow field boundary left. (Be aware that this wood is used by some as a 'meeting place', so best to keep your dogs and children on the path and try to stop them picking up 'odd' pieces of litter.)

6 **Turn left** through marked gap in hedge and stay with hedge to RHS for two fields, crossing road on to side road ahead. At end, **turn right** into field. Now keep alongside left boundary through gates and fields to track. **Ahead** on to road (both path and driveway on left lead to church which may be visited if desired). After passing rear of Dyrham Park house, **go left** through gate immediately before the lodge. Climb track to junction, **turn right** to road then **left** to retrace the outward route uphill: steps **left** into woodland, **ahead** alongside deer fence, metal gate, stone stile and **right** back along the A46 to the start.

HINTON HILL

KISSING GATE BY ST CATHERINE'S COURT

18 St Catherine's Court & Little Solsbury Hill

15.3km/9.5miles

Up and down, back and forth along two stream valleys, a disused airfield and Little Solsbury Hill with a nature reserve and a Tudor manor house thrown in.

Upper Swainswick » Charmy Down » Holts Down » Chilcombe Bottom » St Catherine's Court & Church » St Catherine's Brook » Northend » Little Solsbury Hill » Upper Swainswick

Start

Park in lay-by on slip road off A46. GR: ST 762683.

Travelling south, leave A46 signed *Langridge Bailbrook Swainswick* and it is 50m on your right; travelling north, leave A46 signed *Langridge Tadwick Woolley Swainswick* and keep left to pass underneath A46 then lay-by is on the left. (There is also parking on the A46 southbound just before the turn-off.)

The Walk

A climb along a well-made track leads to Charmy Down airfield; in operation from 1941 to 1945 it is now used for cattle grazing. Leaving the plateau, a field walk along the edge of woodland is followed by a drop into Chilcombe Bottom. The reservoir constructed here in the 1840s went out of use in the 1980s and Wessex Water has created a wetland nature reserve: an information board is erected by the exit.

After climbing past a market garden, a narrow, winding road leads to St Catherine's Court, formerly owned by actress Jane Seymour; no expense has been spared then or since in maintaining this grade I listed manor. St Catherine's Church, adjacent, is open. Drop to St Catherine's Brook and the Limestone Link path which joins the Cotswolds to the Mendips, but after going south for just three kilometres leave the stream and climb through Northend.

It is a twisting, often-muddy path through ancient woodland that leads on to Little Solsbury Hill, made famous by Peter Gabriel. Occupied as a hill fort during the early Iron Age, the summit is now owned by the National Trust. The late walker may get the (Bath) city light, but no eagle is likely to fly out of the night. A short downhill, mostly through fields, returns to the start.

The zigzag nature of this route means confident map readers can take shortcuts if desired, but the full distance allows views across valleys to what is to come or what went before.

ST CATHERINE'S COURT & LITTLE SOLSBURY HILL

DISTANCE: 15.3KM/9.5MILES » **TOTAL ASCENT:** 385M/1,263FT » **START GR:** ST 762683 » **TIME:** ALLOW 4.5 HOURS **MAP:** OS EXPLORER 155, BRISTOL & BATH, 1:25,000 » **REFRESHMENTS:** NONE ON WALK » **NAVIGATION:** STRAIGHTFORWARD; SHORTCUTS POSSIBLE.

ST CATHERINE'S COURT

18 ST CATHERINE'S COURT & LITTLE SOLSBURY HILL
St Catherine's End House
Cripp's Farm
Ayford Bridge
The Hermitage
Summerhill Wood
Motcoombe Wood
Dicknick Wood
Fewells Wood
Quarry (dis)
Coombe Wood
Stillcombe Wood
St Catherine
ST CATHERINE CP
Court Farm
St Catherine's Court
Airfield (disused)
Cowleaze Wood
Charmy Down
Lyegrove Wood
Camp Site (disused)
Holts Down
Wingfield Farm
Cherrywell Wood
Bailey's Wood
Upper Northend Farm
Charmydown Farm
Ramscombe Bottom
Short Wood
Oldhouse Farm
Ppg Sta
The Hill
Reservoir
Northend
Chilcombe Bottom
BATHEASTON CP
Little Solsbury Hill
Fort
Common
Elmhurst Estate
Church Farm
Batheaston
Swainswick Lane
Bailbrook
Lower Swainswick
© CROWN COPYRIGHT AND/OR DATABASE RIGHT. ALL RIGHTS RESERVED. LICENCE NUMBER 100025218.

Directions – St Catherine's Court & Little Solsbury Hill

S Leave the lay-by with it on your LHS and walk uphill, bend left and, just before A46, take No Through Road **right** signed *Public Bridleway.* Continue for 1.2km. Where surfaced track turns sharp right, instead go **ahead** through gate towards barn (there are three PF options – this is the third one). Pass with barn on LHS and continue to gate; **turn right** around perimeter track of disused airfield. Continue for about 750m, passing mast, until level with first line of brick sheds in field on left and where gates and cattle handling set-up forces change of direction. **Turn right** over stile following mud-covered tarmac track alongside left fence, then cross stile **left** but continue on same line in adjacent field. Follow track back **right** towards boundary wall then **ahead** through gate on to walled track.

2 After 450m take PF **right** into field. Aim **half right** for hedge/tree corner then follow this boundary across several fields into narrow beech tree belt by farm. At far side of trees, **half left** across field corner to drive. **Turn right** joining second track, then **left** crossing field diagonally downhill. Locate path at bottom left corner; **ahead** through gap in sparse hedgeline and **ahead again** to stile leading to steps steeply down.

3 At bottom **half right** and down to valley bottom, there picking up track **left** between hedges. Cross road taking permissive path through Chilcombe Bottom Nature Reserve. Again cross road then again **continue ahead** through HG on to PF along lower field edge. Pass two overgrown pumping station sheds then around fallen tree and **left** over bridge/stile. In field, aim **half right** to climb to a KG, cross second field to top corner. At road **turn right** and continue to crossroads. **Turn left.**

4 After approx. 400m uphill, **turn right** downhill on path (adjacent to Bath water treatment works) and **ahead** to road. **Turn left**, and **left again** at T-junction and stay on this road for just over 1km to St Catherine's Court and church.

5 Where railings end, **turn right** through KG then **half left** down and into a garden, crossing corner and streams by FBs, stile into field then **hard right** over another stile; St Catherine's Brook is now on RHS. Aim up field to second then third telegraph poles and ahead to large green box (modern pump housing), picking up a track. Stay on this track **ignoring** stile left and permissive path. Before reaching farmhouse driveway **return right** to valley bottom. Cross FB then follow PF arrows and keep St Catherine's

Brook on RHS, crossing driveways and fields for about 700m until stream and path both meet road in the corner of a field. Exit via stile, and **turn right** on to the road.

6 After crossing stream **turn left** into narrow hedge-lined path and over stile into field. Now **ahead** with stream on LHS to stile. **Turn left**, recross stream, now **right** into field and ahead with stream on RHS. Continue to road. **Turn right** and pass green corrugated iron workshops to T-junction; **turn right**, then **left** at grass triangle and **ahead** up narrow wet path.

7 **Ahead** uphill into Seven Acres Lane, then **left** at PF sign on to track, through KG and **ahead** then **turn left** at field corner to follow first field boundary. At second field **half right** to a dog-leg in the hedge (aim to left of the cluster of trees and large bushes), through a gap in the hedge, path passes between hedges then through gate and along bottom edge of field before stile into private woods with well-defined, if narrow, muddy path through, up and out on to Little Solsbury Hill.

8 **Before** striking out to top of hill, look right. There is a sign and a stile and this is where you will need to come back down. Having climbed this far, complete your climb to the trig point or walk the hill perimeter. Leave Little Solsbury Hill by KG; path following right field boundary until path junction and finger post. **Left** across field to gate and **left** at lane to junction with car ahead.

CHILCOMBE BOTTOM

ULEY BURY

19 Owlpen & Hetty Pegler's Tump 16.3km/10.1miles

Sharp, steep hills, both up and down, with rewarding views, an outstanding Cotswold manor house and a long barrow to explore.

Uley Bury » Cam Long Down & Cam Peak » Downham Hill » Uley outskirts » Owlpen » Nympsfield » Hetty Pegler's Tump » Uley Bury

Start

Crawley Hill (B4066), Uley. Roadside parking by Uley Bury. GR: ST 787993.

The Walk

Follow the Cotswold Way down a steep track from Uley Bury and up, down and around Cam Long Down, Cam Peak and Downham Hill. These are small outcrops from the main limestone ridge of the Cotswolds, and were once surrounded by – if not under – water. Downham Hill was, much later, the site of an isolation hospital, hence the local name of Smallpox Hill. After crossing the valley the route passes close to Stouts Hill, a Gothic Revival house built in 1743 by the Gyde family of local mill owners. From 1935 to 1979 this was a school educating amongst others Stephen Fry and (Capt.) Mark Phillips, former husband of Anne, Princess Royal. It is now marketed as a 'holiday resort'.

The hamlet of Owlpen is best known for its grade I listed Tudor manor house. After eighty years of neglect, it was saved in 1926 with careful Arts and Crafts style repairs. The house and gardens are now open for pre-booked tours, or hired out for weddings, and there are nine holiday cottages available for rent. It is worth a very short detour to visit the Church of the Holy Cross: the stained glass is lovely, but less common are the mosaics and tiling in the chancel and tower.

At the top of the walk is the village of Nympsfield with its church and the Rose and Crown inn (dogs welcome in bar) after which the route again joins the Cotswold Way. The intriguingly named Hetty Pegler's Tump can only be reached by a road out-and-back diversion, but this is one long barrow that the agile can crawl inside. Return to the start through undulating woodland on the Cotswold Way.

For those with too much energy, a stroll around the hill fort and SSSI that is Uley Bury offers another view of the Severn plain, and of some of the places visited on the walk.

OWLPEN & HETTY PEGLER'S TUMP

DISTANCE: 16.3KM/10.1MILES » **TOTAL ASCENT:** 515M/1,690FT » **START GR:** ST 787993 » **TIME:** ALLOW 6 HOURS
MAP: OS EXPLORERS 167, THORNBURY, DURSLEY & YATE, & 168, STROUD, TETBURY & MALMESBURY, BOTH 1:25,000
REFRESHMENTS: ROSE & CROWN, NYMPSFIELD » **NAVIGATION:** STRAIGHTFORWARD.

WEST FROM COALEY PEAK

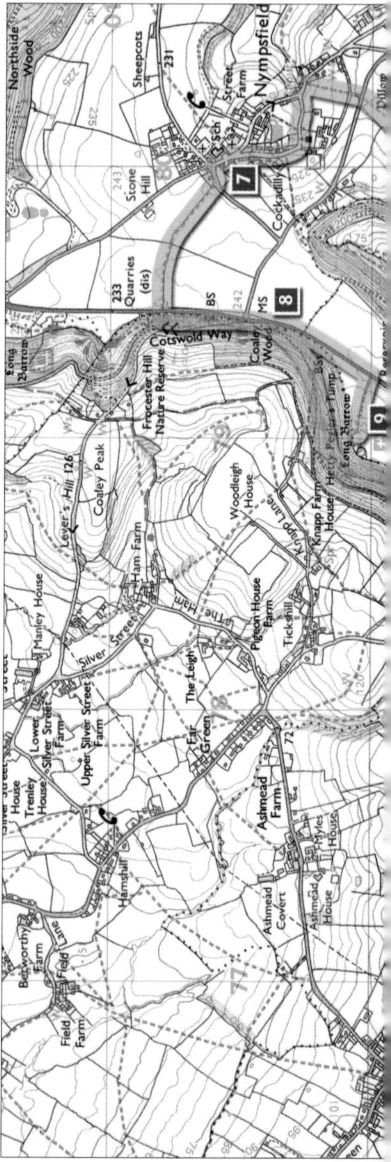

19 OWLPEN & HETTY PEGLER'S TUMP

Directions – Owlpen & Hetty Pegler's Tump

S From the car parking, take the **left** track (Cotswold Way) steeply downhill, following round left after it passes through Hodgecombe Farm and flattens out. **Turn right** at the road; the hill you are about to climb is ahead, so at right bend in the road go over stile on **left** and **straight up** on to Cam Long Down. Continue climbing through trees after stile and at top continue to highest ground on right with views over River Severn and beyond. Follow ridge along then follow track down to fingerpost, walking **ahead** signed *Cam Peak*. Climb up and down the other side, turning **left** on to path before reaching the garden hedge (and **ignoring** 'ahead' arrow). There are several paths, all go roughly the right way but best to work down until the fence is close to your RHS. Round the edge of Cam Peak then **right** through a kissing gate, and down the field to the road.

2 **Straight across** on to PB which is parallel to drive. This may be very muddy (the tarmac drive with CGs may be easier walking). Stay on tarmac after CGs through gate on **left** and between barns through yard. At the other side go **left** over stile and cross field diagonally toward barns, leaving field over another stile and on to track. Follow track round bottom of Downham/Smallpox Hill to junction. Keep on main track bending first right then keeping downhill to meet road.

3 **Straight across** into driveway of Sheephouse Farm. Go **straight ahead** to end then follow arrow **right**, over stile, bearing round **sharp left** on to track. Before stables walk **half right** to top corner of field (around pond) over stile. **Turn left** and go **straight ahead** to meet a track and road. **Turn right** at *Restricted Byway* sign and stile leading steeply up into woods. At the path junction, **hard left** and stay on path close to edge of wood for just under 1km looking for a stile **left** leaving wood (just before meeting wide tracks left and right). Walk down and **right** in field, aim for a double stile where there is a view across to Stouts Hill.

4 Follow left hedge to corner then **straight ahead** in field to large, lone oak tree from where you will see a KG ahead. Now **half left** between trees to stile in bottom fence then **half right** aiming to left of Lye Farm house. Follow driveway to road and **turn right**. Opposite postbox **turn left** over stile into field. **Ahead** to stiles into second then third field, look for (and use) stile into field on **left** but continue on same line. Over four stiles in quick succession then **half right** to stile in field corner. Now **ahead** and up to next stile then **turn left** along lower hedge to road. **Turn right**.

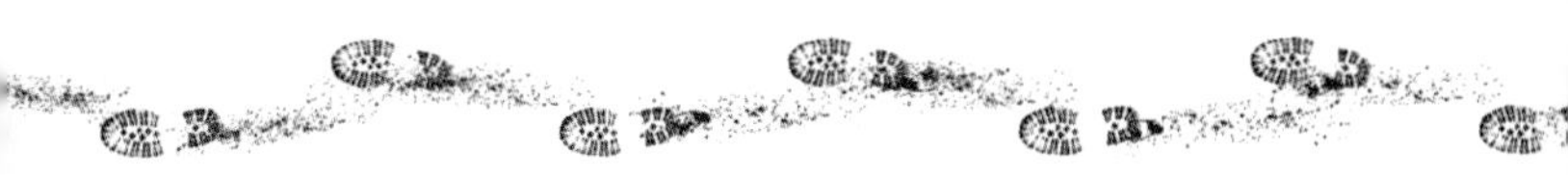

5 **Walk uphill** to sharp RH bend, entering field on **left** at PF sign. Diagonally downhill, then around to **left** into next field. Aiming to left of church, locate stiles to reach bottom corner of field, through young trees to road. **Turn right** and continue around LH bend. To visit church **turn hard right** signed *Owlpen Manor*.

6 Return to the road and **turn right** and uphill. Continue until road turns left and down; here go **ahead** on to track signed *Owlpen Woods*. **Straight ahead** on level main track through several gates/stiles. After approx. 1km track bends sharp right. Leave track on **left** on or after bend (exactly where depends on temporary fencing and mud!) to continue along valley bottom with woods on both sides, before following gentle curve **left** to stile at edge of wood. Through woods, steeply uphill; over stile ahead to leave woods, then cross via gateway/broken stile (maybe it will get mended) into field on right. Keep fairly close to LH hedge to a stile by the gate. **Cross road** on to short track opposite, then **ahead** over stone stile and down into Nympsfield. **Turn left** at road and **left** again to pass church. Keeping **ahead**, Rose & Crown pub is on the left.

7 Continuing in same direction, take road **left** and after house **turn right** on to track then into field. **Ahead** over stile, continue to road. **Cross with care** and take footpath **right** then **left**, now on Cotswold Way to Coaley Peak. Continue through damp woodland to road. Again cross, going uphill and round to right.

8 Stay on road, passing Cotswold Way sign (you will return this way). **Continue with care** on roadside for about 450m. Path to Hetty Pegler's Tump is on the **right**: it is possible to avoid much of the road walking although there are no footpaths through adjacent fields.

9 After exploring the barrow, backtrack to point 8 and **turn left** on to Cotswold Way, following undulating path through woods to the start. (It is also possible to just continue along the road from the Barrow, but it isn't a pleasant road for walking.)

WORCESTER LODGE HUNTING PAVILION ON WORCESTER AVENUE

20 Badminton

16.7km/10.4miles

A flat route with a mixture of roads, bridlepaths – which tend to be muddy – and fields. Typical pretty Cotswold villages punctuate the walk.

Bullpark Wood » Little Badminton » Badminton Park » Great Badminton » Park Pale » Luckington » Sopworth » Bullpark Wood

Start

Parking at side of unclassified road, 1km south-west of Didmarton. GR: ST 813866.

The Walk

Do not attempt this walk in the first week of May when the horse trials are taking place as the entire area will be gridlocked.

At first follow bridlepaths on the Duke of Beaufort's Badminton Estate. As well as the horse trials, this is home to the Beaufort Hunt and also gave its name to the game of badminton. The estate includes Ragged Castle folly (grade II* listed but falling/fallen into disrepair) and Worcester Lodge, a hunting pavilion built in 1746 which is visible from the main house over four kilometres away. Both can be seen during the walk, though they need to be looked for. Continuing on roads through farmland to Little Badminton where, as on much of the walk, most of the farms and cottages are owned by the estate, the route then goes through the deer park where glimpses of Badminton House can be seen between the trees and on into Great Badminton, passing close to the hunt kennels with their associated sounds and smells.

Also heard but unseen, trains travelling between London and South Wales pass through the now-disused Badminton Station close to Acton Turville. Park Pale, originally the site of a paling fence at the edge of the old deer park, leads seamlessly across the boundary into Wiltshire where the route passes a rough mound on the right. This is the Giant's Cave, a Neolithic chambered long barrow where the remains of twenty burials were found. There is no public access and, as can be seen, the features are overgrown and indistinct.

In Luckington village the tin Methodist chapel opened in 1903 with a congregation of 200 for their first service. The Old Royal Ship is welcoming but does not admit dogs, although there is ample room outside. Across fields to the village of Sopworth, then track and more field paths back to the start.

BADMINTON

DISTANCE: 16.7KM/10.4MILES » **TOTAL ASCENT:** 135M/443FT » **START GR:** ST 813866 » **TIME:** ALLOW 5.5 HOURS **MAP:** OS EXPLORER 168, STROUD, TETBURY & MALMESBURY, 1:25,000 » **REFRESHMENTS:** VILLAGE SHOP/PO, GREAT BADMINTON; THE OLD ROYAL SHIP, LUCKINGTON » **NAVIGATION:** FOOTPATHS MAY BE UNCLEAR THROUGH WOODLAND AND PONY PADDOCKS.

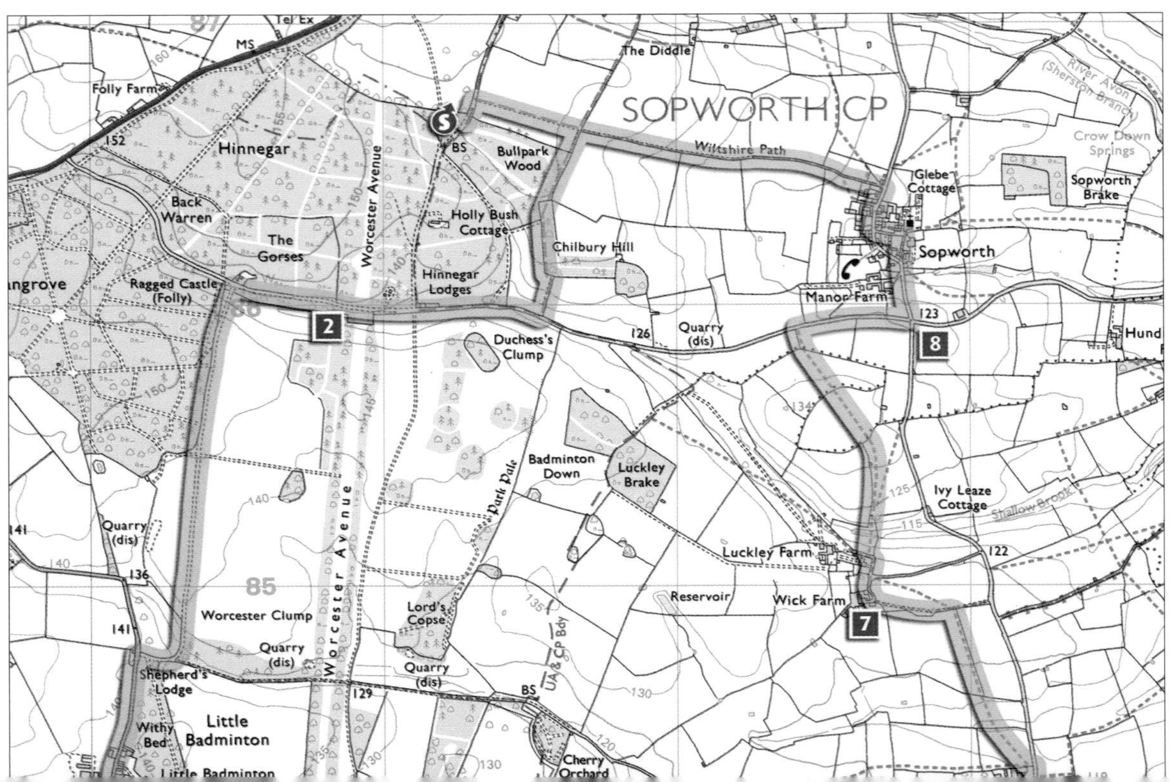

Tel Ex
MS
The Diddle
River Avon (Sherston Branch)
Folly Farm
SOPWORTH CP
Crow Down Springs
152
Hinnegar
BS
Bullpark Wood
Wiltshire Path
Glebe Cottage
Sopworth Brake
Back Warren
Worcester Avenue
Holly Bush Cottage
Chilbury Hill
Sopworth
The Gorses
Hinnegar Lodges
Ragged Castle (Folly)
Manor Farm
123
2
126
Quarry (dis)
8
Hund
Duchess's Clump
150
134
Badminton Down
Luckley Brake
Park Pale
140
125
Ivy Leaze Cottage
Shallow Brook
141
Quarry (dis)
115
136
Luckley Farm
122
85
Reservoir
Wick Farm
135
Worcester Clump
Lord's Copse
141
7
UA & CP Bdy
Quarry (dis)
Quarry (dis)
Shepherd's Lodge
129
BS
130
Little Badminton
Withy Bed
120
Cherry Orchard
Little Badminton

20 BADMINTON
Badminton Park
Deer Park
Badminton House
Badminton
Vicarage Plantation
Badminton Farm
Cape Farm
Centre Walk Brake
Fatting Barn
Park Pale
Giant's Cave Chambered Long Barrow
Allengrove Farm
Allengrove Lane
Allen Grove
Quarry (dis)
Hermit's Cell
Mounds
The Mount
Oak Plantation
Mount Pond
Park Pond
Splash Pond
Hebden Farm
Hebden Leaze
Hebden Leaze Farm
Macmillan Way
Alderton Grove Farm
Alderton Grove
Pit (dis)
Badminton Station (disused)
Centre W
Withy Moor
Quarries (disused)
Quarry (dis)
BADMINTON CP

Directions – Badmonton

S The road from Didmarton runs north–south with the woods at the southern end: leave the road and walk **east** into the field with the boundary of the wood on your right. At end of field **turn right** through wood, following PB as straight ahead as possible to a road. **Turn right**. **Keep ahead** at junction. At wide ride a quick detour up the bank on the right will reveal Worcester Lodge; this can be seen from Badminton House, which is cleverly obscured in the opposite direction.

2 **Ahead** to grass triangle noting Ragged Castle folly in trees on right. **Turn left** through stone gateposts and **ahead** following road right round bend after about 1.5km. Between more stone gateposts, **turn left** on road. **Proceed with care** to **turn left** into Church Lane, passing the church of St Michael and All Angels, Little Badminton, on left and medieval grade II* listed dovecote in field on right. **Turn right** at the VR postbox and **left** at next junction through grey wooden deer gates, noting seasonal warnings about dogs and deer.

3 Keep on this road/track through the parkland. At the end of the park, take the gateway on the **left** of the two. At the road junction, go **ahead** into Hayes Lane with the two-tone yew and privet hedge on the left. **Turn right** then **left** at the junctions and continue along the road for nearly 1km. Passing the *Acton Turville* and *30 mph* signs, follow the road left past the cottage, then **turn immediately left** on to the track.

4 The path continues across fields with the field boundaries on the left. After passing small wood on left and upon entering a very narrow field, **do not** go ahead through HG. Instead take the FG **left** and now continue **ahead** with the hedge on RHS. Through gate into the next field, go **half left** looking for brick piers (once barn roof supports) over hedge ahead, then through gateway just to their **left**. Now aim for dead tree in middle of field from which the gate ahead is now obvious. **Turn right** on to road. **Turn left** at crossroads.

5 Passing overgrown Giant's Cave in field on **right**, take the second gate on **right** following PF sign **half left** across field where there is a gap in the hedge to the right of the three oak trees. In this next field go **left** to aim to LHS of overgrown dewpond

in centre of field. Continue to FG and **ahead** on to road. Pass Allengrove Farm and in and out of a small dip, then, where the road can be seen to bend left, **turn right** over a somewhat overgrown stone stile at PF sign. Continue to end and through gate ahead. You are now faced with two post-and-rail fences across the path. Looking ahead and slightly left is a conifer hedge; the path passes to the left of this. To get there you must now either climb over or through these two fences, or follow the rails right then back left. At the LHS of hedge, go through gate, then **keep left** against circular wooden enclosure under apple tree towards roof, keeping mobile home on right. Narrow path leads between sheds and stone walls to emerge on The Street in Luckington. Post office and shop is immediately opposite. **Turn half left** on to main road towards tin Methodist chapel and on to the Old Royal Ship public house.

6 **Turn left**, keeping pub on RHS. **Turn right** into Sopworth Road, pass Northend, a small road on LHS, then at the end of wall, look for PF sign **left**. Path climbs steps into a field where the route goes **half right** to a barely visible stile. At next field, angle across to a gap just **right** of the oak tree and follow field boundary **ahead**, crossing stile then **left** on track.

7 **Turn right** in front of house, and **ahead/left** at junction to LH bend where path drops into field **ahead**. Over clapper bridge and **straight ahead** up field on far side to gate. Keep to LHS of field to end then **right** for a few yards where the Cotswold Wardens have (as of 2016) placed a new if slightly awkward stile. **Ahead** to cross field between trees to gateway, then in next field **ahead** again, keeping to right of lone oak to gate and along short track to road. **Turn right**.

8 At crossroads **turn left** into Sopworth. At LH bend take narrow PF **ahead** between walls to another locked church. Leave via Church Lane, then **right** at end, passing cottages. **Do not** take first path left but, after passing the barn on the RHS, look for Wiltshire Path Cottage on LHS, then **turn left** on to Wiltshire Path. **Keep ahead** with hedges to left. At field go **left** and **right**, still keeping hedge and then wood to left, to reach road at the start.

LOOKING SOUTH FROM ULEY BURY (ROUTE 19)

1 DAY WALKS IN SCOTLAND

LOCH LOMOND & THE TROSSACHS

available 2018

By Svenja Timmins

2 DAY WALKS IN SNOWDONIA

20 CIRCULAR ROUTES IN NORTH WALES

By Tom Hutton

3 DAY WALKS IN THE BRECON BEACONS

20 CIRCULAR ROUTES IN SOUTH WALES

By Harri Roberts

4 DAY WALKS ON THE PEMBROKESHIRE COAST

20 ROUTES IN SOUTH-WEST WALES

By Harri Roberts

5 DAY WALKS IN THE LAKE DISTRICT

20 CIRCULAR ROUTES ON THE LAKELAND FELLS

By Stephen Goodwin

6 DAY WALKS IN THE YORKSHIRE DALES

20 CIRCULAR ROUTES IN THE CENTRAL PENNINES

By Bernard Newman

7 DAYS WALKS IN THE NORTH YORK MOORS

20 CIRCULAR ROUTES IN NORTH YORKSHIRE

By Tony Harker

8 DAY WALKS IN THE PEAK DISTRICT

20 CLASSIC CIRCULAR ROUTES

By Norman Taylor & Barry Pope

9 DAY WALKS IN THE PEAK DISTRICT

20 NEW CIRCULAR ROUTES

By Norman Taylor & Barry Pope

10 DAY WALKS IN THE COTSWOLDS

20 CLASSIC CIRCULAR ROUTES

By Judy Mills

11 DAY WALKS IN DEVON

20 CIRCULAR ROUTES IN SOUTH-WEST ENGLAND

By Jen & Sim Benson

12 DAY WALKS ON THE SOUTH DOWNS

20 CIRCULAR ROUTES IN HAMPSHIRE & SUSSEX

By Deirdre Huston

Appendix

The following is a list of Tourist Information Centres, shops, cafes, pubs, websites and other contacts that might be useful.

Tourist Information Centres

www.cotswolds.com – Official website for Cotswolds tourism.

Bourton-on-the-Water T: **01451 820 211**
E: **info@visitbourton.com**
www.bourtoninfo.com

Broadway T: **01386 852 937**
E: **info@beautifulbroadway.com**

Burford T: **01993 823 558**
E: **burford.vic@westoxon.gov.uk**

Chipping Campden T: **01386 841 206**
E: **info@campdenonline.org**
www.chippingcampdenonline.org

Cirencester T: **01285 654 180**

Painswick T: **01452 812 278**

Stow-on-the-Wold T: **01451 870 998**
E: **stowvic@gloucestershire.gov.uk**
www.stowinfo.co.uk

Winchcombe (seasonal opening) T: **01242 602 925**
E: **winchcombetic@tewkesbury.gov.uk**

Wotton-under-Edge (limited opening)
T: **01453 521 541** E: **wuehistsoc@gmail.com**
www.wottonheritage.com

Food and Drink

Cafes

(See individual routes for recommendations.)

Adlestrop Post Office: T: **01608 659 475**
The Ark Coffee Shop
Wotton-under-Edge T: **01453 521 838**
Bourton-on-the-Water: various options
Broadway: various options
Morris & Brown Cafe
Broadway Tower T: **01386 852 945**
Painswick: various options
The Tollgate, A46
Dyrham T: **01225 891 585**
Winchcombe: various options

Village Shops

Adlestrop Post Office T: **01608 659 475**
Drewett's Store
Badminton T: **01454 218 212**
North Nibley Shop T: **01453 548 374**

Pubs

The Bell at Sapperton T: **01285 760 298**
The Black Horse Inn
Naunton T: **01451 850 565**
The Black Horse Inn
North Nibley T: **01453 543 777**
The Craven Arms
Sevenhampton T: **01242 820 410**
The Daneway Inn
Sapperton T: **01285 760 297**
Falcon Steakhouse
Wotton-under-Edge T: **01453 521 894**
The Golden Heart Inn
Birdlip T: **01242 870 261**

The Greedy Goose
A44/A436 T: 01608 646 551

Hunter's Hall Inn
Kingscote T: 01453 860 393

King's Head Inn
Bledington T: 01608 658 365

The Kingsbridge Inn
Bourton-on-the-Water T: 01451 824 119

The Lamb Inn
Great Rissington T: 01451 820 388

Old Royal Ship
Luckington T: 01666 840 222

The Plaisterers Arms
Winchcombe T: 01242 602 358

The Plough Inn
Cold Aston T: 01451 822 602

The Queen Elizabeth
Elmley Castle T: 01386 710 251

Rose & Crown
Nympsfield T: 01453 860 612

The Royal George Hotel
Birdlip T: 01452 862 506

Seven Tuns
Chedworth T: 01285 720 630

The Slaughters Country Inn
Lower Slaughter T: 01451 822 143

Snowshill Arms
Snowshill T: 01386 852 653

The Swan at Southrop T: 01367 850 205

Tunnel House Inn
Coates T: 01285 770 280

Victoria Inn
Eastleach T: 01367 850 277

The Woolpack Inn
Slad T: 01452 813 429

Weather

www.metoffice.gov.uk

Outdoor Shops

Attwoolls
Bristol Road, Whitminster
T: 01452 742 233 www.attwoolls.co.uk
(Also stock a vast range of camping and caravanning supplies.)

Cotswold Outdoor
Cotswold Water Park, South Cerney
T: 01285 863 930 www.cotswoldoutdoor.com

Cotswold Outdoor
Abbey Gate Street, Bath
T: 01225 562 230 www.cotswoldoutdoor.com

Go Outdoors
Barton Street, Gloucester
T: 0344 387 6828 www.gooutdoors.co.uk

Other Publications

Day Walks in the Brecon Beacons
Harri Roberts, Vertebrate Publishing –
www.v-publishing.co.uk

Day Walks in the Peak District
Norman Taylor & Barry Pope,
Vertebrate Publishing –
www.v-publishing.co.uk

Cotswolds Mountain Biking
Tom Fenton, Vertebrate Publishing –
www.v-publishing.co.uk

About the Author

Judy Mills' love for the English countryside grew when she moved to a small Somerset village at the age of nine. After studying ecology at university, she found that jobs where she could sit in a field counting flowers were hard to come by, so spent thirty years in the police service, leading voluntary working holidays with the National Trust in her spare time.

A keen but slow runner she completes a couple of marathons each year as well as taking part in the annual Cotswold Way Relay. She enjoys walking and horse riding, and in 2014 cycled from Land's End to John o'Groats. She lives with her husband in Gloucestershire where they keep sheep and beef shorthorn cattle.

About the Photographer

Adam Long is a Sheffield-based photographer, specialising in images of wild landscapes, the nature that lives there, and the way people interact with them. His work has been widely published, by publications and clients including *The Times*, National Trust, UKClimbing.com and the British Mountaineering Council.
Find out more: **www.adamlong.co.uk**

Vertebrate Publishing

At Vertebrate Publishing we publish books to inspire adventure.

It's our rule that the only books we publish are those that we'd want to read or use ourselves. We endeavour to bring you beautiful books that stand the test of time and that you'll be proud to have on your bookshelf for years to come.

The Peak District was the inspiration behind our first books. Our offices are situated on its doorstep, minutes away from world-class climbing, biking and hillwalking. We're driven by our own passion for the outdoors, for exploration, and for the natural world; it's this passion that we want to share with our readers.

We aim to inspire everyone to get out there. We want to connect readers – young and old – with the outdoors and the positive impact it can have on well-being. We think it's particularly important that young people get outside and explore the natural world, something we support through our publishing programme.

As well as publishing award-winning new books, we're working to make available many out-of-print classics in both print and digital formats. These are stories that we believe are unique and significant; we want to make sure that they continue to be shared and enjoyed.
www.v-publishing.co.uk